Moon Up
Moon Down

BOOKS BY JOHN ALDEN KNIGHT

The Modern Angler

The Theory & Technique of
Fresh Water Angling

Ol' Bill

Modern Fly Casting

Woodcock

Field Book of
Fresh-Water Angling

Ruffed Grouse

Black Bass

Fishing for Trout and Bass

Tecnica del Lanzado

The Complete Book of
Fly Casting
(with Richard Alden Knight)

John Alden Knight
fishing one of his favorite Pennsylvania trout streams

"It is the fate of all truths that they begin as heresies."
CARDINAL RICHELIEU

Moon Up Moon Down

By

John Alden Knight

SOLUNAR SALES CO.

MONTOURSVILLE, PA 17754

2001

Originally published by
CHARLES SCRIBNER'S SONS
Copyright 1942

Revised edition by
JACQUELINE E. KNIGHT
SOLUNAR SALES CO.
Copyright 1972

Second revised edition by
JAMES C. AND LINDA J. LOSCH
SOLUNAR SALES CO.
Copyright 2001

ISBN 0-9716385-0-0

Library of Congress
Catalogue Number:
72-93383

*To Beth and Dick
whose faith has never wavered*

FOREWORD

THE ownership of an inquiring mind often is a dubious asset. Not always does it pay to be too curious. But when an inquiring mind and an unquenchable conscience are combined, then indeed does the owner find himself frequently in hot water.

First knowledge of what is now called the Solunar Theory was acquired by accident. That would have been all right if the matter had rested there and the knowledge been used in the form in which it first was gained. Once having learned, however, that this new bit of outdoor lore was even more useful than I had supposed it could be, the everlasting and ineradicable question, "Why?" kept popping up until it could no longer be denied.

Even then no serious consequences could have arisen if I had been content to keep my findings to myself. That is where the conscience entered the plot. Knowing that other sportsmen and, for that matter, mankind in general would be better off for having access to what had been learned, there was nothing to be done but make truthful confession of the entire matter. Then events followed upon events until we had difficulty in keeping up with them.

First off, do not be dismayed by the high-flown name of the Solunar Theory. Formidable as it may sound, it is merely a convenience term, coined in self-defense, so that discussions could be carried on with the minimum of cumbersome verbiage. Briefly, the Solunar Theory can be summed up in this way:

Other conditions not being unfavorable, fish will feed, animals will move about, birds will sing and fly from place to place, in fact, all living things will become more active, more alive, during Solunar periods than at other times of apparent equal value.

That's all there is to it, all you need to know in order to understand how the Solunar Theory affects you and all living things about you every day that you live.

Please understand that this is no attempt to write a scientific treatise on a newly discovered natural law. Quite the reverse, it is merely a recounting, in the language of the layman (of which I am one, although I hold a university degree) of the development of the schedule of Solunar activity periods and of how the development of that schedule has warped the destinies of the Knight family. To that is added a discussion of the many ways in which the habits, lives and, in some cases, the very existence of living creatures are affected by the promptings of a natural law which, for some strange reason, has hitherto escaped identification.

It is probable that you will not agree with all that is contained herein. For that I am sorry. Nevertheless, the only way to tell a story is to tell it in full. Half-truths are of little value. What is said has been said in all humility and in the sincere belief that the Solunar Theory will, eventually, be of benefit to mankind.

JOHN ALDEN KNIGHT.

Moon Up
Moon Down

CHAPTER ONE

THE brown waters of Lake Helenblazes lay glassy and still under the Florida sun. It was July and the St. Johns River marshes fairly quivered with the midsummer heat. Now, at eleven-thirty, we had taken refuge in the scanty shade of a little camphor tree that somehow had found its footing on one of the floating islands that drift about the surface of the lake—the only tree in all that desolation of rushes, reeds, water hyacinths and swamp water.

We had been fishing for large-mouth bass since dawn. Usually the fishing in "Blazes" was excellent, but throughout the morning, the bass had been unresponsive. Tiring of fruitless casting, we had knocked off for an early lunch.

As we sat there, Bob Wall, my guide, looked at his watch and then out across the surface of the lake. The heat waves had built a mirage that lifted the horizon above its normal level so that it seemed to hang in midair, leaving a gap of clear, shimmering nothing between itself and the quiet water. I could see that Bob was restless. Finally he spoke.

"Come on, Jack," he said. "Hurry up with that lunch. We'll miss the good fishin' if we sit here much longer."

"What makes you think they'll rise in all this heat?" I asked him.

"They'll rise, all right," he answered. "Moon's down about noon."

"Whats that got to do with it," I said.

"Never mind about that," said Bob. "Just take my word for it. These fish are goin' on the feed pretty quick now."

"You'll have to think up a better one than that," I told him, "to get me out in that heat again. This is the first time I've been anywhere near comfortable for the past four hours."

Bob shrugged his shoulders and told me the story while I munched sandwiches and drank cold tea. His "granpappy" had been a market hunter and fisherman in South Georgia when Bob was a youngster. From him Bob learned fishing and hunting. Among other things, the old man had told him that the time to go after fish or game is when the moon is directly overhead or directly underfoot. The men who made their livelihood selling game and fish, while such things were still legal, all recognized the effect the moon had on the creatures of the wild, and their hunting and fishing trips were planned according to daily moon positions.

I listened to Bob's story with more interest than he suspected. Ever since I was a boy, fishing for sunnies and chub in the small streams near my home in Pennsylvania, I had wondered about the manner in which fish would bite ravenously at some times of the day and ignore our choicest offerings at other times of that same day. As I grew older, the mystery still persisted. I had made it a point to question the older and more experienced fishermen but they could throw no useful light on the subject. About all that I had gained from many hours of such conversations was a rather formidable mass of conflicting misinformation. This idea of Bob's was the first useful peg upon which one might, possibly, hang his hat.

Accordingly, I choked down the rest of my lunch and we went fishing under the broiling rays of the July sun. Never in my wildest dreams have I seen such bass fishing as we had that day. I remember that my first cast was made into the waters of a tiny cove, well fringed with reeds and protective water growth. The white plug dropped to the surface with a light splash and lay there, motionless, while concentric circles of wavelets spread themselves away from it. After a few seconds, I raised the rod tip to tighten the line and bring the plug to life. At the first twitch of the rod, the plug dipped its nose under the surface and bobbed up again. With that the quiet waters of the cove were burst asunder by the furious strike of a mighty bass. Surprised, I struck back with the rod, but the weight of the big fish tore the reel handle from my fingers. The spool spun and threw out loops of line that intertwined themselves into a "bird's nest" of magnificent proportions. When order was restored, the fish, of course, was gone and the plug floated once more on the placid surface of the cove, just as if nothing had happened. Bob spat, eloquently, over the side.

"Now," he said, "mebby you'll settle down and do a little fishin' for a change."

That was the beginning of almost three hours of hysteria. We hooked fish, big fish. Some we landed and some we lost. We broke lines, skinned knuckles, lost plugs, laughed, yelled and cursed. How many fish we caught and released, I do not know, certainly more than we had ever caught before. That evening we hung on the boathouse scales that part of our catch we had brought out with us—nine large-mouth bass that totaled seventy-eight pounds.

Meanwhile, I had forgotten about Bob's "moon-up—moon-down" theory. Not until I was in my car and on my way home did I remember it. During the five-hour drive back to Orlando, I had plenty of time to reconstruct the whole experience.

Bob had predicted that our good fishing would begin about noon. Sure enough, that's when we had the real activity, particularly with the larger fish. After about two hours of superlative fishing, the action began to slow down until, at about three o'clock, things were almost as quiet as they had been during the morning. Then, along toward evening, there had been another flurry of activity and we had taken an eight-pounder at the inlet of Lake Washington.

I suppose that fish will linger in my memory always. We were waiting at the inlet for the other boat to show up and Bob suggested that I cast a plug out over the swifter water where the river flowed into the lake. Although I had done almost enough fishing for one day, I decided to try my luck again, more to help kill time than with any real angling enthusiasm. Having cast across the raceway, I allowed the plug to drift quietly with the current before starting the retrieve. It swung in a wide circle below the boat and, as it nearly completed its swing, it was taken with a quiet, solid strike, so typical of a feeding fish.

At first I could not move the heavy bass from his position in the fast water. He just sulked against the pull of the line, much as a fighter feels out his antagonist in the first round. Then he bore for the bottom, taking line, where he sulked again in about fourteen feet of water. Almost without warning he changed tactics. With a rush he charged straight for the surface and his momentum carried him up into the air, where he seemed to hang, while the crimson glow of the sunset tinged his silver side with red. It was a picture not easily forgotten. The background of the St. Johns marshes already were tinted with the exaggerated colors of the Florida sunset and against this exotic backdrop hung the giant bass, both he and the silver spray of his splash touched with the magic brush of evening.

All this and the validity of Bob's prediction filled my mind as I drove my car homeward across the flat miles of central Florida. I wondered if the "cracker" market hunters were right about wild life timing its feeding periods by the moon instead of the sun. I decided to find out.

For the next few years I checked, off and on, Bob's theory of "moon-up and moon-down." At some times of the month, the feeding periods arrived right on Bob's schedule. At other times, there was considerable variance. Having neither the time nor the opportunity to make regular observations, not a great deal was learned during those years and the formation of an accurate schedule still remained a mystery, although I felt sure that I had the key to the problem.

One evening, while pondering on the variance of the "moon-up—moon-down" theory with the true schedule of feeding periods, I considered the possibility of finding the prompting stimulus by the process of elimination. Accordingly, I made a list of everything I could think of that might have its effect upon the feeding habits of both fresh and salt water fish. Before I had finished, I had itemized better than thirty factors that would, perhaps, influence fish in one way or another. Temperature, water condition, availability of food, movement of water, barometric pressure and so on down through the whole gamut of possibilities until I could think of no more.

Then, with the list as complete as I could make it, I considered each item in the light of its effect, if any, upon *cyclic* feeding periods. In so doing, it was obvious that the stimulus must be of an external nature and not immediately and exclusively present in the water itself. This reasoning was based upon the proven fact that feeding activity occurred in all parts of a stream, lake, ocean, or, for that matter, in *several different bodies of water at the same time*. If this stimulus were confined to the waters of one particular section, this concurrence of activity would not be possible. Viewed in this light it seemed reasonable to conclude that the prompting stimulus was of a general rather than a local nature.

As each factor of the list was considered and rejected, it was crossed out. When I had finished, all of the factors but three had been crossed off as impossible. The remaining three had question marks after them, indicating doubt with room for further examination. These three were "sun," "moon" and "tides."

The sun, of course, is the heavenly body by which our time is calculated. It makes its appearance in a regular and well-ordered manner, whereas the feeding periods of fish are apt to show up at any time and rarely at the same time on any two days. It couldn't be the sun.

The moon had already been tested and found wanting for at least a part of the month.

Tides—well, there are no measurable tides in a pond or a trout stream.

And there I was, right back where I had started.

Sitting there, looking at the useless list of factors, an idea came to me.

Ocean fish time their feeding periods according to tidal phases. Tides are caused by the gravitational pull of the moon and the sun. Could it be possible that fresh-water fish time their feeding periods on the same schedule as that used by their ocean cousins? The idea was certainly worth investigation.

Obviously, if the tidal theory were to be investigated, it was necessary for me to learn something about tides. The best place to obtain accurate information is at the source. Accordingly, the next morning found me in the New York office of the United States Coast and Geodetic Survey. At that time, Commander George D. Cowie was in charge of the New York office. In response to my request to have a talk with the gentleman in charge, I was shown into his private office.

"Commander Cowie," I said, "I would like to learn something about tides."

"Yes," he said politely, "just what do you wish to learn?"

"Assuming that our Atlantic coast line lay in Illinois instead of New Jersey, I want to find out how I can figure out what time it will be low tide at Chicago."

Commander Cowie looked startled.

"I beg your pardon?" he said.

Then I started at the beginning and explained my problem. If fresh-water fish, living in lakes and streams far removed from the Atlantic Ocean, time their feeding periods according to the tidal schedule of the Atlantic tidal basin, then for me to calculate the schedule of their daily feeding periods, I must be able at least to understand how tidal times are figured out. Knowing that, I should be able to go on from there under my own steam. Commander Cowie nodded and smiled understandingly. Before I realized what had happened, he was saying good-bye to me at his office door, having supplied me with tide tables, Geodetic Survey maps, and Marmer's excellent book on tides. He seemed quite relieved to see me depart while I was still semi-rational. As a matter of fact, when I came to know him better, he admitted that he was a trifle dubious as to my complete sanity that first day in his office.

My years of salt-water fishing had taught me that the best feeding time for salt-water fish is at low tide. That statement should be qualified somewhat. In bays, river mouths, and inlets, where tidal flow is hampered somewhat by natural obstructions such as bars or shoals, the feeding period is apt to arrive at most any stage of tide. But where the waters are situated so that the tidal phases are those of the *true schedule* of the Atlantic tidal basin, then the time of low tide marks the active feeding period. This made a rather loose method of approximation, as slack water lasts for as long as two hours, but at least it was a place to start. Assuming that Sandy Hook (at the suggestion of Commander Cowie) was most likely to represent the true Atlantic tidal schedule, unaffected by obstructions to natural flow, I added ten minutes to the Sandy Hook tidal times (to allow for the difference in longitude between Sandy Hook and the streams of Eastern New York State and Eastern Pennsylvania) and this schedule went with me when I found the chance to go on fishing trips.

To my great satisfaction, this schedule came closer to the actual feeding schedule than Bob Wall's "moon-up—moon-down" schedule had done. It was far from perfect but it was close enough to show that I was on the right track.

That summer Mrs. Knight and I had accepted an invitation to fish the waters of a trout stream owned by a fishing club in Connecticut. Saturday was a hot, windless day and the trout were moving not at all. My schedule showed me that a feeding period was due at about three o'clock that afternoon and my son (a little fellow then, but an ardent angler) and I had gone downstream, leaving Mrs. Knight in the car, which had been parked in the shade near the bridge. Her reading was interrupted by the arrival of another member of the club. She watched him fish the pool under the bridge, the pool above and the one below. Not a single trout came to his offerings. At last, disgusted, he reeled in his line and came over to the car for a chat.

"Too hot and clear today," he said. "The trout won't move in weather like this. Where's Jack?"

"He and the boy have gone downstream," she answered. "He said he wanted to be on those lower pools when the feeding period came in."

"What feeding period?" he asked.

She explained my idea about low tide. The club member had quite a laugh over it.

"That's the craziest thing I ever heard," he said, looking at his watch. "But it's twenty minutes before three now. I think I'll stick around and see what happens."

So saying, he sat down in the shade, leaned against a tree and lighted a cigarette. At three o'clock he arose, picked up his rod and walked out on the bridge. His first cast netted him nothing and he smiled knowingly as he put the fly up over the pool again. This time there was a flash of spray, and he was fighting a fourteen-inch trout almost before he realized what had happened.

After landing this fish, he detoured around the bridge pool and entered it carefully from the lower end. In ten minutes, two more hefty trout lay in his creel. Then he came back to the car.

"Do you really think there's anything to this low-tide idea of Jack's?" he asked Mrs. Knight.

"Jack says there is," she replied. "You fished those pools carefully only forty minutes ago with no results."

The club member scratched his head.

"How long," he inquired, "does this low-tide feeding period last?"

"Usually about an hour and a half or two hours," she replied.

He nodded thoughtfully and walked up the path along the stream. Some time later he returned with a fine basket of trout.

For obvious reasons, I did not talk too much about my new feeding schedule. Radical ideas of this sort are not always welcome among the more seasoned anglers, and I wanted to be sure of my ground. All of that season I checked my schedule against the actual feeding periods. Not only did I make my own observations but, by judicious questioning, I learned that the experiences of other anglers nearly always coincided with my own. I found that the schedule of low-tide times was close enough to be a great help in planning each day so that the best fishing would not be missed.

That winter threw no new light on the subject. As a matter of fact, I did not put too much time on it. After all, it was at that time merely an interesting side light on my favorite hobby and I had my regular job to take care of. The following season found me continuing my observations, however, still using the same method of low-tide calculation. It was during this season that I learned of the cycle of intermediate feeding periods that occur midway between the major, "low-tide" activity periods. Conveniently, these periods seemed to be timed concurrently with the schedule of Sandy Hook high-tide times and I kept track of these also. More and more I became convinced that I was on the right track of what constituted a natural law of cyclic activity. While I did not know it at the time, science has known of this cycle for some two hundred years. I was to learn more of that later.

During the fall of that year I attended an anglers' dinner given by one of my friends. Eugene V. Connett, III, was one of the guests also. At that time he was on the board of the magazine, *The Sportsman*. During cocktails, he asked me if I was turning out any articles for the outdoor magazines. I said that I was writing one now and then.

"How about doing one for us on that low-tide idea of yours?" he said.

Then and there we sat down and came to an agreement as to price, details, etc. The next day I started work in earnest.

In evolving the theory of "inland tides" and their effects on the feeding habits of fish, it must be remembered that this was an attempt to work out a law, rule, formula or method by starting at the result and, by trial and error, guessing my way back to the possible cause. All I had to go on at that time was the fact that ocean fish and, probably, inland fish, time their feeding periods concurrently with tidal phases. Feeling that the flow of the tides themselves was responsible in some way for the phenomenon, I attempted to reconcile the tidal intervals of the Atlantic tidal basin with those of the Pacific coast. This was a sad mistake, as it threw the schedule completely awry in the states located in the central part of the country. Fortunately an engineer in Indiana was smart enough to spot this fallacy and bring it to my attention before too much damage had been done. It all came about this way.

The theory of "inland tides" was first made public property in January, 1935, in the article written for *The Sportsman*. In it I explained the fundamental idea of the tidal theory. When the Geodetic Survey wishes to determine the tidal intervals of a certain section of coast line, a recording machine is installed which automatically keeps a record of tidal fluctuations at that port. This machine is operated for one or two years before tide tables for that particular section are calculated in advance. The reason for this preparatory period of observation is to enable the Geodetic Office to determine, without doubt, the tidal lag in those waters—in other words, the interval between the actual time of the passage of the *cause* of the tides (the pull of the moon and the sun) and the arrival of high tide. This tidal lag, occasioned by the inertia accompanying the movement of the Atlantic tidal wave and the attendant flow of water over natural obstructions, is known as the "high-water interval" or, for brevity, the H. W. I. of that port. The H. W. I. of the Atlantic basin itself is, roughly, six and a half or seven hours. That of the Pacific basin is almost three times that. Thus, in attempting to graduate these theoretical H. W. I.'s for inland waters across the country, you can readily see how much confusion would result.

All this was explained carefully in that first article. In order to facilitate description, the theory was given a name. Tides being caused by the sun and the moon, I combined the words "solar" and "lunar." Thus was the Solunar Theory born.

The response to the article in *The Sportsman*, (which, incidentally, was called "Ocean Tides and Fresh-Water Fish") was surprising. Letters came in from nearly every state in the union, requesting more detailed information. I replied to as many of these letters as I could, and in April, 1935, another article, amplifying that of January, was published in *The Sportsman*. Then, to top this off, articles on the same subject were published in both *Field and Stream* and *Outdoor Life*. Without question, the sportsmen of the country were introduced to the Solunar Theory.

Slowly at first, but with increasing volume, letters from readers began to come in to the editors of the three magazines. Editors believe that "fan mail" should be answered and these letters were forwarded to me for reply. At first, I did the best I could with them, but I was finally snowed under. To have answered all of those letters in detail would have required the services of not less than five stenographers and my full time to do the dictating. What, then, to do about it and still keep everybody happy?

Sitting at my desk one evening with that staggering pile of mail before me, a possible solution of the problem came to mind. After all, with a few exceptions, the writers of the letters wanted to know the same thing—where or how could he, or she, obtain a schedule of the feeding periods of fish in the waters of his, or her, section of the country? The next day I went to the printer and had some postcards printed. On these cards I stated that for the sum of fifty cents, to cover the cost of printing, mailing, etc., I would forward to the sender a booklet listing the Solunar feeding periods for each day of the season in all parts of the country. Then I had a thousand books printed and sat back to see what would happen. The first thousand books lasted just five weeks.

Meanwhile my job in the city was not an easy one. At that time I was engaged in doing some special work in downtown real-estate brokerage for the bank where I was working. That meant long hours and hard work. Up at six-forty-five each morning, I was on the go until I returned home, usually about seven each evening. Not having too much time for detail work at home, I made a deal with Beth, my wife. I agreed that if she would fill the orders, attend to the mailing and pay for the postage out of her part of the proceeds, she could have all of the actual cash that came in. Checks, money orders and stamps belonged to me. I can still see her standing on our veranda as the postman handed her the daily mail, shaking each letter to see if it rattled. We had a lot of fun that season.

The postman, who had reached the stage of becoming "an institution" on our street, watched the volume of our mail grow, in a short time, from a daily trickle of three or four letters to a twice-daily flood. Eventually his curiosity could stand it no longer. Having unloaded his sack at our door one morning, he removed his hat, scratched his head and said,

"Excuse me, Mrs.; I know it's none of my business but I can't help wonderin'. A month ago you was gettin' three-four letters a day and a few mags. All of a sudden, mail comes pourin' in here 'till I get round-shouldered carryin' it. Just what the hell is goin' on?"

Beth explained just what the hell went on. He nodded, scratched his head again, and walked slowly down the walk as though thinking to himself, "Now why can't I think of somethin' like that?"

After that we had an interested third party in business with us. Before he handed over the mail, *he* shook it first with some such comment as, "Heavy this mornin' —feels like plenty of cash, too"; or, "Not so much this time. Better get *him* to write another story."

As the money continued to come in and we had to order more books to be printed, it dawned on us that this influx of orders might not be a temporary thing but an annual event. Without realizing it, we were in business for ourselves; you might say, kicked into it.

CHAPTER TWO

Having a new source of income practically dumped in our laps was a timely and pleasant surprise. Things had not been going too well for the Knight family. What with the '29 "crash," the shrinkage in security values and the complete collapse of downtown New York real-estate brokerage, the family exchequer had dwindled rapidly. We moved from Westchester to Orange, New Jersey, and tried to cut down on family overhead. That's pretty hard to do. I had found a job with one of the big banks but that meant long and regular hours at about 20 per cent of the money I had earned formerly. Magazine articles helped somewhat, but the going was still fairly tough.

That summer, with the aid of checks from the magazines and the sale of Solunar Tables, we traded in our old car and bought a new one. With the advent of fall, we found that we had turned in quite a respectable income. Accordingly, we sat ourselves down and made plans.

Beth and I made another deal. After all, most of my time was taken up with my work in the city. On the other hand, this looked like a chance to get back on an independent basis again. She agreed to handle all the detail work in connection with the sale of the books—mailing, card files, desk work, etc. To my lot fell publicity, correspondence, advertising and finances. It looked like a busy winter ahead.

In order to sell anything, no matter what it may be, the more you know about it the more chance you have to sell it. That's just plain common sense. I made up my mind that if the sales of Solunar Tables were going to amount to anything of importance, it was up to me to find out about the formation of a more accurate schedule. More important, it was my job to discover, if possible, just *why* this phenomenon should take place.

Correlations are dangerous things to play with if you are serious about the job in hand. The Sophists found that out some thousands of years ago. For instance, day in and day out you may have dinner at six each evening. It does not necessarily follow that, just because it happens to be six o'clock, you will, without fail, sit down to dinner.

Some years ago a senior in one of our universities chose as the subject of his senior thesis the topic of correlations. Perhaps the most lasting portion of that work is what he termed "the straw-hat correlation." Through dint of thorough and painstaking investigation he built up a conclusive and bullet-proof relationship between the number of straw hats that find their way each year into the garbage cans of New York City and the number of pneumonia cases that show up in the New York hospitals. After a year of research, he set up a beautiful equation that showed a set, mathematical ratio between these two unrelated annual totals. As one number increased, the other increased in proportion and *vice versa*.

Obviously, the contributing factors—the catalyzers—are those of temperature fluctuations and weather changes. But these need not be considered in order to have his correlation stand the test, year after year.

Thinking about these things, it seemed to me to be just as far-fetched to believe that ocean tides, of themselves, could possibly have any direct effect upon the lives and habits of fresh-water fish in streams and lakes far removed from the ocean. Carried a step farther, it seemed almost as inconclusive that the rise and fall of the tides could be the complete controlling factor governing the feeding cycle of salt-water fish. How can a bluefish, for instance, swimming ten miles offshore with half a mile of water under him, detect a change of depth of three or four feet and thereby regulate his entire daily routine? Could it be possible that the correlation by which salt-water fishermen have planned their days since the year one—the belief that certain stages of tide control the feeding habits of fish—is, also, a high-grade bit of sophistry?

From knowledge gained on past fishing trips and from questioning several ardent salt-water anglers, I learned the stages of tide at which the fish bite best at nearly all of the well-known angling concentration points on the Long Island and New Jersey coasts—Montauk Point, Moriches Bay, Fire Island Inlet, Toms River, Beach Haven and so on. Then, from the tide tables, I set down the *actual times* that the critical phase of tide arrived at these key points on one particular day. Plotted on a sheet of graph paper, the curve of tidal phases made no sense at all. But the curve of the times of arrival of those tidal phases turned out to be almost a straight line. In other words, these good fishing times at the various bays, passes, rivers and inlets arrived *all at the same time*. If the best time to fish at Montauk Point happened to be 2.30 P.M. on a certain day, then 2.30 P.M. was the best time to fish at Beach Haven or Toms River on that same day, regardless of the fact that the stage of tide differed in all three places. Salt-water fishermen have been guiding their efforts for hundreds of years by a rule that is substantially as groundless as the "straw-hat correlation."

The timing of the feeding cycle for both fresh and salt-water fish being synchronized with that of tidal fluctuation, the next possibility, in natural sequence, was a closer look at the conditions that are the cause of the tides—the gravitational pull of the moon and the sun.

In terms of actual work done, the moon is boss man in that combination, exerting, as it does, approximately twice the amount of influence exerted by the sun. Just to see how it would work out, I tried making up a Solunar schedule by determining the resultant of the two forces—the pull of the moon and the pull of the sun—and using as the Solunar period the time that this resultant force was directly applied to our particular longitude—either overhead or underfoot. The minor periods were placed midway between these major Solunar periods because that is where I had learned, from observation, to expect to find them. This schedule proved to be more satisfactory than the one concocted from the use of tidal times, although it still was far from being exact.

Shortly after the publication of the four articles introducing the Solunar Theory, I was approached by the head of a publishing house that specializes in textbooks. He had an idea that it would be good business to publish a series of textbooks dealing with the finer points of the various outdoor sports, such as fresh-water angling, salt-water angling (if you can call it angling), yachting, waterfowl shooting, upland shooting, fox hunting, riding and so on. These works were not to be in any sense elementary; in fact, they were to be postgraduate courses in the selected sports. He wanted me to do the book on fresh-water angling. I agreed and, just to complicate matters completely, I found myself writing a comprehensive manuscript for a fishing book. Meanwhile we had gone ahead with the second edition of the Solunar Tables. Work grew heavier for both of us and bedtime moved from midnight to one or two o'clock.

The textbook publisher changed his mind about the publication of his series of works on the outdoor sports, so the manuscript was reshaped somewhat and, in April, 1936, was published by Charles Scribner's Sons under the title *The Modern Angler*. To get the book off to a flying start, the publicity department at Scribner's arranged for me to speak at the "Headliner's Luncheon," held each week at the Downtown Athletic Club in New York City. I had never addressed a gathering of more than a few people and the prospect of speaking to an assemblage of over four hundred persons had me just about scared to death. Going up in the elevator to the big dining hall, my knees fairly trembled. At the speaker's table my palms were moist, my collar tight and my mouth dry. Although I had prepared my notes carefully, they had little or no meaning as I looked at them on the table before me. Then, in desperation, I gave myself a pep talk. These people, I told myself, probably don't know as much about fishing as you do and nothing at all about the Solunar Theory. Talk to the smartest man in the room. You know more than he does about your subject matter. Sell him on the idea that you know what you're talking about and you won't have any trouble with the rest of them. When I was introduced and found myself standing before the microphone of the loudspeaker system, I found that I was fairly cool and collected. My talk was scheduled for thirty minutes. It must have gone over all right as they had me on my feet for about an hour and forty minutes. I never did get a chance to eat my lunch.

That summer found me feeling pretty rocky physically. I suppose that the years of the depression, with the attendant loss of money and reduction of income, combined with recent loss of sleep and too much work, all united to take their toll on my physical reserve. The bank doctors looked me over, as did my own doctor and a couple of specialists. All agreed that there was nothing wrong organically but that I was well run down and needed a rest. Accordingly, Beth, my son and I climbed into our car and headed for Maine with instructions from the doctor to "come back when you feel well enough to go back to work." I returned in September, feeling greatly refreshed and went back into the old routine again.

During the spring and summer I had had only an occasional opportunity to make personal observations on the accuracy of the Solunar schedule. Obviously, this was a tremendous handicap. In order to form any conclusive ideas, the schedule should be checked each day throughout the fishing season. Having a living to earn and a job to earn it with, I had to stick to that job and work on the Solunar schedule when I found the chance.

I tried to enlist the aid of others in making observations for me, but that proved unsatisfactory. For some reason, only about one man in a hundred is mentally equipped to see things intelligently. I received many reports and tried to coach volunteer observers in what to do and what to watch for. Finally I gave it up as a bad job, as the reports received were, in the great majority, practically useless. I could see plainly that I would have to do the job for myself. Men who were scientifically trained had their own axes to grind and those without that training were of little or no help.

Looking back, I can see that this inability to be on the stream every day retarded the development of an accurate schedule more than I realized. At that time, however, nothing could be done about it. We just made the best of it and went ahead building our little business as well as we could. Then, out of a clear sky, loomed some information that opened up a new field of research.

CHAPTER THREE

It IS a strange thing, in working on a phenomenon of this kind, how items of information, which mean little or nothing at the time they are gathered, sooner or later fit themselves into the big jigsaw puzzle. Having learned this from experience, I have become what Beth calls a mental pack rat. Every week I receive letters from users of the Solunar Tables here and there about the country. Frequently, there are odd bits of information in these letters. While these may have little or no significance at the time, most of them serve a purpose eventually.

Take, for instance, the effects of the trend of the barometer on the behavior of wild life. In 1925, while reading F. G. Shaw's book, *The Complete Science of Fly Fishing and Spinning*, I saw therein a statement to the effect that the dry fly was more effective on clear, sunny days, while in wet or threatening weather a wet fly, fished deep, was preferable. There it was—one man's observation of the types of flies to use during good and bad weather. That bit was stored away in my mental filing cabinet for future reference.

Some years later, I began to wonder about the reputed effect of wind direction on the habits of fish. For the life of me I couldn't understand how a fish could know—or why it would care—which way the wind happened to be blowing. One day, just for the fun of it, I analyzed the old saw that has been used by fishermen for countless years to forecast their luck. You know it, I'm sure. It goes something like this.

> Wind in the East, fish bite least.
> Wind in the West, fish bite best.
> When the wind is in the North
> The prudent angler goes not forth.
> When the wind is in the South
> It blows the hook in the fish's mouth.

Beliefs of this sort which, like many of the old home remedies, have stood the test of time, often have more to them than may appear on the surface. Let's take a look at this doggerel in the light of barometric trends and weather conditions. "Wind in the East"—harbinger of a falling glass and bad weather along our Atlantic seaboard. The fish take to cover and are not interested in food for the time being. "Wind in the West"—good weather with a fresh breeze and a high or rising glass, probably indicating good fishing. "Wind in the South"—warm, gentle breezes and good weather, with a steady barometer. No wonder the fish go on the feed. "Wind in the North"—as a rule this is a strong, cold wind, shifting to the east. That means adverse temperatures and a falling glass. Obviously bad weather for fishing.

To carry this thought farther, I kept track of the barometer and its effects on fishing for a year or two.

It all tied in with Shaw's idea about the best flies to use in good and bad weather. I found that a drop of as little as one one-hundredth of an inch in the level of the barometer would often ruin the fishing. Not having a pocket barometer (they were pretty expensive then), I used instead some of the old country "signs" to tell me what the glass was doing. Leaves turning upside down in a light breeze, the "rain song" of a robin, more-than-usual noise and activity among the blue jays—all of those things would tell me when the glass was falling. Checked against my barometer and the government weather reports, the "signs" proved to be accurate enough for practical everyday use. Even the behavior of the fish was a good indication. A hurried, smashing strike usually denotes a fish that is not feeding actively. A feeding fish will generally take with a confident, unhurried rise that is unmistakable. Before two seasons had passed, the effects of the barometer were proven beyond doubt, at least to me.

In the May issue, 1935, of *Outdoor Life*, an article of mine was published under the name of "Fish Know Their Weather." In this article the effects of barometric trends on the feeding habits of fish were discussed. At that time I attached no particular importance to the "barometric theory," as it is now called, feeling that it was more or less common knowledge. That was a mistake. Two years later I received from a gentleman who was connected with one of the Midwestern universities a rather exhaustive report, complete with graphs and tables, showing that the level of the barometer actually does have its effect on the feeding habits of fish. Incidentally, this gentleman explained, in that same letter, just why the Solunar Theory is a fallacy and of no practical value.

In 1939 I received a letter from an editor of one of the outdoor magazines calling to my attention an article that was being published in his magazine in the coming issue. He thought I would like to know about it as it dealt with the "new" theory of the effects of the barometer on the feeding habits of fish. All this, mind you, after this very thing had been included in the introduction of the Solunar Tables since January, 1936. In *The Modern Angler*, published in April, 1936, there was a complete discussion of the same phenomenon. I couldn't help smiling when I considered that I had sent to that editor a pre-publication copy of *The Modern Angler*. He must have enjoyed every word of it.

This may seem fairly far removed from the Solunar Theory. That is what I thought at the time the data on the barometer were being collected. Instead, it all fits into the pattern very nicely.

About the time that these things were happening, I chanced upon the condensed version of an article in one of the monthly magazines. Without quoting from it, the substance of it is this:

Surrounding us in the atmosphere at all times are tiny electrical particles called ions. These may be attached to microscopic bits of dust, to droplets of water, to each other or they may be in the free state. Also, all matter that surrounds us—the earth, trees, houses, water—absorbs, to its complete capacity, these tiny electrical particles. They are divided primarily into two classes—those that are positively charged and those that are negatively charged. Each class is subdivided into several groups according to size, intensity and mobility.

Our main interest in these ions lies in their effects upon us as individuals. It has been shown, rather conclusively, in the experimental laboratory of one of our large manufacturing corporations, that these little ions play their daily parts in the state of our well-being. Repeated experiments have shown that negatively charged ions have a beneficial effect on living things, while positively charged ions are deleterious.

Being interested in this phase of the article, I drove to the city where the main plant of this corporation is located and, through letters of introduction from our bank, had a talk with the scientist in charge of the experimental laboratory. I found his description of these experiments fascinating.

Two insulated rooms were constructed in the laboratory. To make sure that the results of the experiments would be both rapid and obvious, the atmosphere in these rooms was charged with a supply of ions one million times that of ordinary air. One of the rooms was charged with negative ions, the other with positive ions. At first, plants and flowers were placed in the rooms for varying lengths of time. Those placed in the room charged with positive ions soon withered while those in the negatively charged room seemed to benefit from the experience. Next, small animals such as mice and guinea pigs were subjected to the same treatment. Those placed in the positively charged room seemed to suffer unpleasant reactions from this overdose of positive ions, while those placed in the negative room showed signs of stimulation.

One of the junior engineers in the laboratory, a husky youngster in good physical condition, volunteered his services as a human guinea pig. He was placed in the positively charged room for about twenty minutes. At the end of that time he came out, described his sensations, and was looked over quite thoroughly. His head ached, his temperature had gone up nearly two degrees, his heart action was accelerated to a pace above normal and an old joint injury, sustained in football, throbbed unmercifully. After he had been given time to recover and was back once more to his normal state of good health, he was placed in the negatively charged room for twenty minutes. He came out declaring that he felt like a millon dollars. A checkup showed that he was functioning normally although unquestionably stimulated, much as though he had had a highball or two. Similar experiments were conducted until the effects of the two types of ions were clearly established.

Everyday manifestations of these reactions are common enough. Consider, by way of illustration, how you feel on a sparkling, spring day when the sun is shining, the air smells clean and fresh and the barometer is high or rising. You just can't help feeling good on a day like that. But what is taking place from the standpoint of terrestrial magnetism? As atmospheric pressure increases, the absorption capacity of all the things about you increases and ions are taken up by the earth, trees, houses and so on. Because of the fact that negative ions are more active—possess higher mobility—they soon unite with positive ions and no longer remain in their free, beneficial state. Positive ions, on the other hand, are of lower degrees of mobility and remain free for longer periods of time. Thus, they are always available in their free form to be taken in by all living things. On a day such as I have described, there are fewer of these harmful ions in the atmosphere to be absorbed, consequently we feel fine and the world seems a good place in which to live.

On the other hand, what happens when the barometer starts to fall? As atmospheric pressure decreases, so also does the absorption capacity of the things that surround us. This results in ions being given off into the atmosphere. The negative ions are soon taken out of circulation but the harmful, positive ions remain in their free state, either singly or in groups, ready to be taken up by all living things. Thus, when wet weather is approaching, its coming is announced by the ache of your pet corn or your rheumatic elbow or knee. On wet, foggy days you usually feel below par and there is little energy or enthusiasm in you. It's a perfectly natural reaction.

As soon as the sun goes down, positive ions in the atmosphere become larger and more active and in this form they are capable of doing more harm. Years ago, people not in the best of health were cautioned against going out in the "night air." Bedroom windows were kept closed because "night air" was reputed to be harmful to a sleeping person. Viewed in the light of terrestrial or atmospheric magnetism, our ancestors were not far from being right about night air. It wasn't so long ago that pneumonia patients were kept in cold rooms with the windows open. This treatment was adopted after the "harmful-night air" theory had been exploded. Now pneumonia patients are kept in warm rooms with the windows closed. People suffering from colds or grippe are advised to sleep in warm rooms. It has been learned that in this way they get better faster. Night air has a certain quality about it, a different smell or feel—an intangible something that you do not notice in the daylight hours. And nobody has yet explained to me, satisfactorily, just why it is that my car runs so much better after dark. Neither has it been explained why sound travels farther or why odors are more perceptible at night than they are in the daytime.

This also may seem to be rather far afield from the puzzle of the Solunar Theory and its cause. But it isn't, really; quite the contrary.

In our primary correlation, we have learned that the Solunar schedule times itself according to the movements of the moon and the sun. Some attempt has been made to attribute this timing to changes in atmospheric pressure. Let's take a quick look at that side of the picture.

More or less recently it has been learned that there are atmospheric tides just as there are ocean tides. They follow the moon and the sun more closely, their movement being hampered by less inertia than that of water. However, these tides cause pressure variations so minute that they can be detected only by the more sensitive barographs. An average aneroid barometer is unaffected by them, so far as the eye can perceive. The effects of barometric fluctuations on fish have been attributed to pressure change, *per se*. A change of atmospheric pressure theoretically registers itself on the balance or specific gravity of a fish by altering slightly, through compression or decompression, the size of its "swim sac" (the bladder, filled with gas, that lies next to the backbone). The nervous system of a fish is pretty highly tuned, but I don't think that it can be as accurate as all that.

For purposes of discussion, consider a trout in a pool. Suppose he has taken up his position five feet below the surface. Assume, also, that the barometer has fallen one full inch in the glass. To compensate for this change of atmospheric pressure, all that the trout needs to do is to move his resting station 1.1333 feet closer to the bottom of the pool and he has offset this barometric change completely. To compensate for a drop of one one-hundredth of an inch, all the trout need do is to alter the depth of his position a little less than an eighth of an inch. Yet a drop of one or two hundredths of an inch in the level of the glass often will ruin completely a day's fishing. I have seen it happen many times. Even the wave motion at the surface, caused either by wind or the flow of the current, will produce a continual fluctuation of pressure equivalent to as much as a quarter or a half an inch in the glass, but that has no effect on the feeding habits of the fish that live in the water directly beneath these waves.

To go a step farther, suppose this same trout rises to the surface to take a fly. Throughout the journey through five feet of water, the pressure on its sides undergoes a change of 2.16 pounds per square inch of surface. That is equivalent to a change of a little over five inches in the level of the glass or over one fifth of an atmosphere. Of course, it may be argued that it is possible to hear a clap of thunder and, immediately afterward, the sound of a pin dropping to the floor. On the other hand, animals and birds have no sensitive gas-filled bladders to act as aneroid barometers, yet they too feel the effects of changes in atmospheric pressure. It seems unlikely that absolute pressure changes, of themselves, can constitute the true catalyzing agent either in the effects of barometric changes or the effects of sun and moon positions upon the habits of wild life.

Thus it was that my "pack-rat brain" seized upon the description of the effects of ions upon living things and stored it away for future reference. It seems feasible to put the idea to work in this way.

Existing between the earth and the sun and the earth and the moon are lines of force. Gravitational pull is the way this force is described when applied to tides. Molecular attraction is another name for it. Call it by whatever name you like, this attraction of one body to another unquestionably is electrical. It is the nature of electrical lines of force to have surrounding them their own magnetic fields. A magnetic field either attracts or repels — it cannot be neutral insofar as anything else electrical is concerned. Just keep that in mind for a moment.

From outer space, this old world on which we live sustains a continual bombardment of tiny electrical particles known under the general name of cosmic rays. These tiny bits of electrical energy travel at speeds incomprehensible to us in our conception of the term "speeds." They come pounding in from outer space, through the Heaviside layer, the stratosphere, our atmosphere and then into the earth itself where finally they are stopped and absorbed. Thus is our storage battery kept charged. As these high-speed ions come tearing through outer space toward the earth, they collide with and break up the magnetic set-up of the various layers that surround us, keeping our terrestrial magnetism in a constant state of flux. When they come in contact with a molecule, they burst it asunder, making available, at least for the time being, the beneficial negative ions.

It seems to be highly possible that the cosmic rays may be attracted and concentrated by the magnetic fields surrounding the lines of force between the earth and the moon and the earth and the sun, just as raindrops would be collected and concentrated by a large funnel. Thus, during Solunar periods, they are showered upon us more densely than at other times, contributing their stimulating effect and causing the activity that is so typical of those times.

I was having lunch one day with a scientist whose business it is to conduct systematic research in the field of terrestrial magnetism. To him I explained my theory of cosmic rays being condensed and showered upon us more liberally during Solunar periods than at other times. He regarded me intently for a moment and then smiled.

"Ten years ago," he said, "if you had told me that, I would have grabbed my hat and headed for the door. I don't relish the idea of having lunch with a lunatic. Today, all I can say is that you may be right. From the information that we have now, it would be difficult to prove that you are wrong. My advice would be to go ahead as you are going. At least you are on the right track. Stick to your guns and don't be influenced by any criticism. After you fuss around with it long enough, I'm sure you will find the answer and, more important, be able to prove it."

As we have noted earlier, it seems unlikely that the phenomena with which we are familiar such as pressure changes and gravitational attraction, can be the true causes of the effects of both barometric fluctuations and Solunar influence on the lives and habits of all living creatures. Ions and their known effects very probably are the solution. Certainly they furnish answers to questions that have gone unanswered for generations. Now, all we have to do is to prove our theory. It looks like a big job.

CHAPTER FOUR

INCORPORATING this new theory of absolute cause into the calculation of the Solunar schedule occupied about two years. After all, the Solunar Tables were selling fairly well and they functioned satisfactorily enough to give a man his money's worth when he bought one of them. Not having an opportunity to make daily observations, I felt that it was wiser to proceed slowly than to make any drastic changes in the Solunar Tables, with the possible result of monetary loss because of errors either in theory or in the new method of calculation.

Shortly after the idea of magnetic influence came to me, I was invited to speak at a luncheon of a sportsmen's group in Baltimore. For some time I had been corresponding with one of the doctors at Johns Hopkins Hospital in Baltimore. He happened to be interested in the study of cyclic activity and he attended the luncheon. That evening, he was kind enough to invite me to an informal dinner at his club, where he had assembled such of his colleagues and friends as might be interested in what I had to say. The dinner was delicious and the small talk about the table was entertaining. After dinner we moved into the club lounge and, after a few preliminaries, three of those doctors went to work on me to see if they couldn't get a clearer pic-

Moon Up - Moon Down

ture of both the pros and cons of the Solunar Theory.

A doctor does not become associated with Johns Hopkins unless he is an exceptional man in his branch of the profession. These men were keen, intelligent and well read. Meeting any one of them in a mental tilt on purely neutral territory would be an ordeal I should not care to face. In this instance, however, I had a distinct advantage in that I was familiar with the topic in hand, whereas they were not. I later learned that one of them spent his entire time investigating medical theories for the protection of the profession against unsound remedies and cures.

After the inquisition had been going on for perhaps an hour or more, two friends of mine, one of whom was my host while I was visiting the city, dropped into the club to pick me up and take me home with them. Both of them are laymen but they are ardent sportsmen and for several years had been keen followers of the Solunar Theory. After listening to the conversation for a while and finding out which way the wind was blowing, the more hot-headed of the two spoke up.

"Now you listen to me," he said to my main inquisitor, calling him by his first name. "I know nothing of the scientific aspects of Jack's theory and I don't care a damn about that part of it. He's doing the job on that and that's for him to worry about. This much I do know. Any man who will take the trouble to check up on the Solunar periods for a year, *and keep a record* of his observations, has a big surprise in store for him. If he doesn't find that the Solunar Tables will do all that

Jack claims for them and more besides, then I label him as too big a fool to be allowed loose in the outdoors with a fishing rod or a shotgun."

Up to that time, I really do not believe that these men realized that they had been making the going a little rough. They, being actively engaged in the same general work that I had been doing, naturally had doubts about my findings—somewhat different from their own—and they were making the best of the opportunity to clear up their doubts by asking questions. We all laughed at my friend's defense of my efforts and the party settled down to its earlier status of pleasant and congenial conversation. I enjoyed all of it, even though they kept me fairly busy for a while.

That winter my speaking engagements piled up in earnest. Throughout the metropolitan area there are hundreds of sportsmen's clubs and these are always on watch for speakers who will help liven up their meetings and dinners. From the 1st of December until the 1st of May, I spoke on an average of three and a half times a week. This, combined with the work at my desk —which seemed to pile up faster than I could take care of it—and my regular job in the city, kept me on the jump about twenty hours a day. Week-ends were devoted to catching up on my work at home. Sleep became both a luxury and a novelty. I suppose that burning the candle at both ends consumed more energy than I realized because, by the time spring arrived, I was about played out.

The doctors at the bank looked me over and shook

their heads. Nothing organically wrong, but decided debilitation and slated for a breakdown unless something were done about it. One day the senior physician called me on the phone and asked me to come to his office. He told me that it was his opinion, as my physician, that it would be to my best interests to find employment that would keep me outdoors. He impressed upon me the fact that my run-down condition was far more serious than I realized and that if I continued to work indoors I probably would not live more than three or four years more.

That evening Beth and I had a long talk. I told her what the doctor had told me and we debated about ways and means of earning a living. Finally she said, "There's really no use talking about it any more because there isn't anything to decide. It has been decided for us. You hand in your resignation tomorrow. We'll get along, somehow."

The next morning, bright and early, I turned in my resignation and by noon I was no longer an employee of the bank. Having more free time than formerly, I went to work on the Solunar Theory in earnest. After all, the sale of Solunar Tables and articles for the outdoor magazines constituted my sole source of income. It was up to me to pin down the Solunar schedule so that it couldn't miss.

I learned quite a lot about the Solunar Theory that summer. Without question, the method I had been using to calculate the schedule was not entirely satisfactory. In revamping the method, still working from observed effect back to possible cause, it was necessary for me to make daily observations. We were still living in Orange, New Jersey, and it is a long drive from there to the good fishing grounds of the Catskills or the Poconos. Not being able to use fish as my "proving ground," I adopted the expedient of observing all wild life—songbirds, squirrels, rabbits and so on.

A large vacant lot, liberally covered with huge trees and heavily overgrown with underbrush, lay directly behind our house. Its area was about that of two full city blocks. This lot was a concentration point for the wild life of that section. I never knew, when I roamed along its overgrown pathways, just what sort of wild creature I would see next. Quail and dove nested there to my definite knowledge. I have flushed pheasant and woodcock from its thickets, right in the heart of the thickly populated suburb. And the songbirds abounded, literally by the thousands.

From our screened veranda, I could keep track of what went on in "the lot," and the activity among the wild life was as indicative as that in a trout stream or a lake. Not until the damage had been done did I learn that this method of observation was not practical if I wished to obtain the key to the true schedule.

Reaction to Solunar influence (whatever that may be) is peculiar in that all creatures do not react to it in the same manner. Promptness of reaction seems to vary in direct proportion to the order of development. To be more specific, the higher the degree of development, the slower that creature is to react to the stimulus. An excellent example of this variance in response is to watch a Solunar period "come in" in a pool of a trout stream. An hour before the activity period is scheduled to arrive, the surface of the pool is usually quiet, unbroken by the "dimples" of feeding fish. Another of the peculiarities of the activity cycle is that the time immediately preceding the arrival of a Solunar period is generally marked by a term of pronounced inactivity. If you are careful to take your position beside the pool so that the light comes from over your shoulder, you can see the bottom of the pool directly in front of you almost as though the water were not there.

The first sign of activity is among the insect life on the bottom. Stream-bottom nymphs will be in evidence on top of the stones where none were some few minutes earlier. Even hellgrammites, usually to be found only on the under sides of the stones, can be seen moving about in search of food. Next come the little freshwater crayfish—"crawdads," the bass fishermen call them—and they too move about over the stream bottom. Soon the shallows along shore will be filled with schools of minnows, these same shallows having been empty of visible life not half an hour before. A glance over the placid surface of the pool shows a drifting insect or two. Then comes the dimple of a feeding fish. Another, and another! Gradually the pool comes to life. The trout are moving now. There was the rise of a big fellow over by the far bank. Time to unlimber the fly rod and get to work. The high spot of the day has arrived.

With birds and small animals, the delay is even longer than with game fish. Dogs, cows, deer, the larger predatory animals and, finally, humans react even on a more delayed schedule than the lesser creatures such as birds and small game. Thus, in setting up a schedule of Solunar periods, definite consideration must be given to the order of development of the creatures to which the schedule is to be applied. Between the schedule that would apply to insects, for instance, and the one designed for application to humans there is a difference of about two hours in the time of arrival of each activity period. Thus, by timing the schedule with observations of activity among birds, the times calculated for the Solunar periods were sometimes an hour late so far as activity among fish was concerned. It pays to make haste slowly.

During the first summer of my forced semi-retirement from active business, I naturally looked about for some means of augmenting a none-too-adequate income. While pondering on the subject, it occurred to me that a lecture course in one of our metropolitan universities might be an excellent idea both for the university and for me. Armed with a letter of introduction, I journeyed to Morningside Heights and had a brief chat with one of the top executives of Columbia University. And when I say "brief," I mean just that. My suggestion to include in the university curriculum a lecture course on fresh-water angling was met with a polite smile and raised eyebrows. Almost before I knew it, the interview was over and I was on my way to talk to another one of the university authorities. Eventually I found myself in the office of Professor James C. Egbert, Director of University Extension. Realizing that it was now or never, I presented my case to Professor Egbert rather strongly. I argued that students were being trained in the art of earning a living in one way or another. They were being taught how to work. The Department of Physical Education instructs them in the more active competitive sports, few if any of which are useful to the average man after he has been out of college for ten years. In other words, students are being given one-sided training. What I proposed to do was to make available a lecture course which would, through the medium of fresh-water angling, aid the graduated student in his more thorough appreciation of the outdoors in his leisure hours. I would teach him how to play intelligently.

After giving the matter consideration, Professor Egbert decided to install my lecture course in the Department of University Extension. When he announced his intention, he met with stubbon resistance on the part of some of the university authorities. Others joined him in championing my cause. For several weeks the battle waged back and forth, undecided. Finally Professor Egbert and I won out and the course was announced for the coming winter. The newspapers seized upon the announcement and made a great to-do over it. Cartoonists lampooned us in good-natured kidding, columnists took us over the hurdles and the staid *New York Times* ran an announcement in a "box," if you please, in the upper portion of the front page. I don't suppose that ever again I will make the front page of *The New York Times*. Lowell Thomas, number one news broadcaster and an ardent angler in his off time, devoted some time to the course in one of his broadcasts. All-in-all, we kicked up quite a lot of excitement.

The course was given, not in a classroom but in an auditorium that seats one hundred and sixty persons. Attendance varied. The forty-eight enrolled "students" came regularly enough to the fifteen weekly lectures, but I never knew how many more to expect. For two of the lectures every seat was filled, with the overflow sitting on the steps in the aisles. With the aid of blackboard sketches, articles of equipment, motion pictures and a casting exhibition in the gymnasium, I tried to keep my talks lively and interesting. I must have been successful, because attendance did not fall off. At the close of the course, all of the enrolled students received "diplomas" and I was given a contract for a repetition of the course the following year.

The final lecture was shortened to half an hour and then the "commencement exercises" were held. I explained to the class that I was fully aware that a valedictorian customarily is chosen because of his excellence in scholastic standing. In this case, however, there being no final examination, I had no means of telling who had the highest standing. Therefore, lacking this information, I explained that I had gone to the other extreme. We were fortunate, in a way, in having among us a man who was notorious among the anglers who knew him. His claim to fame lay in the undisputed fact that rarely, if ever, did he catch a fish of any kind. Thus, in appointing him as valedictorian, I felt sure that nobody's feelings would be hurt except, perhaps, those of the valedictorian himself.

The victim of this plot accepted the appointment in the right spirit and proceeded to give a remarkably amusing and well-chosen address. The diplomas were given out by the attractive daughter of one of the members of the class and the course came to an end.

The next season it was repeated. In addition, I conducted a similar course in the Adult Educational Group at the Orange High School. Almost one hundred men and women were enrolled in the latter.

Meanwhile one of the editors of Harcourt, Brace & Co., book publishers in New York City, wrote to me advancing the idea that there ought to be a pretty good fishing book hidden in the lecture notes of my course at Columbia. We had lunch together in town and he then "borrowed" me from Scribner's to do the book for him. The following spring and summer found me busy with that manuscript.

One of the big oil companies engaged me to do a fishing folder for them to use in their advertising. What with the proceeds from this, an advance royalty check on the book, income from the two angling courses and my regular business at home, the Knight exchequer once more took on a more healthy aspect.

Meanwhile my real job, perfecting and refining the Solunar Theory, was suffering. War had broken out in China and in Europe and affairs looked extremely uncertain. With the increase in war news in the papers and on the radio, our business began to fall off alarmingly. Folks don't take time to read the advertising in the magazines when each day brings more and more ghastly news of international depredations. We held a meeting of the ways-and-means committee, consisting of Beth and myself.

In Williamsport, Pennsylvania, there was the house where I lived when I was a boy. I still owned it. Why not put it in comfortable condition and live in it? Almost overnight we decided to move, and in September, 1940, we were installed in our new quarters in my old home.

The move to Williamsport was, I feel sure, the smartest thing we had done since we started our new business. At first we were somewhat apprehensive over the possible effect that such a change might have on our income. Fortunately, we need not have worried. Our first year in new quarters showed an adequate sale of Solunar Tables. This and reduced living expenses helped to take up the slack occasioned by the loss of income from various outside sources such as the two lecture courses in angling.

The new book, titled the same as the course at Columbia, *The Theory and Technique of Fresh Water Angling*, was published in September, 1940. During the next ten months I completed the manuscripts of two more books, together with several articles for the outdoor magazines. Whereas I had been working top speed in the metropolitan section, life now slowed to a pleasant, leisurely pace. I had time to devote to the things wherein my greatest interest lay.

CHAPTER FIVE

ONCE established in our new quarters, I hired a secretary to relieve me of the drudgery in the office and began the renewal of my acquaintance with the streams I had fished when I was a boy. Inquiry indicated that there was no fishing to speak of, but I thought I'd look it over just the same. More in the mellow mood of reminiscence than for any other reason, I drove up to a bass pool that had been a favorite of mine thirty-five years ago. A new concrete road had been stretched out across the fields, but the old road still wound its way along the bank of the stream. Facing the pool were several summer cottages, but they were closed and I felt that I had things pretty much to myself. The water not being suitable for bass bug, I screened a supply of hellgrammites out of the riffle. For a stream that was heavily fished, I noticed that there seemed to be plenty of bait left in the fast water. I came home that evening with half a dozen fat bass. Not bad for a stream that was fished out.

There being so much to do at home that fall, getting the house in living condition, my time for fishing was limited. In the few trips I took, however, the story was always the same. There seemed to be enough bass in the neighborhood to keep me pleasantly occupied.

The hunting that fall was another surprise. For many

years the conservation department of the state, working in conjunction with the sportsmen's groups, had been stocking ring-necked pheasants in the surrounding country. Now, a "ringneck" is a big bird, easy to hit, beautiful to display to the family and neighbors and excellent on the table. He makes a great trophy for the farmers (who don't fancy wasting shells) and for the once-in-a-while hunters. I found that the hills and woods were practically deserted and my grouse shooting was done almost without meeting any other gunners. Almost everybody hunted pheasants. A very high percentage of the hunters in this section don't know what a woodcock is and are not interested in finding out. I had an exceedingly enjoyable fall.

During the winter I worked more or less diligently. When spring rolled around, I had the decks fairly well cleared for action and the coming of trout season found me on the stream every day. I did not lack for trout water. Within two hours' drive of my house are no less than fifty good trout streams. My first trip was taken with only a little of the usual, "opening-day" enthusiasm, as I had been told to expect poor fishing. To my delight, I took an even twenty trout within the space of four hours. Most of them were returned to the water, but I brought in six that varied in length from fourteen to eighteen inches. And I had been given to understand that our streams were pretty well fished out.

The most astonishing part of the whole affair, however, was the lack of competition I met on our streams. Being used to the crowded condition of the Catskills and the Poconos, I couldn't become accustomed to having so much outdoors all to myself. During the week, mile after mile of beautiful trout water would lie there before me, totally deserted. Only on four or five occasions was my fishing disturbed by other fishermen.

At first I was unable to account for the lack of congestion on the larger streams and the plentiful supply of fish in them. Now the answer seems clear. Not very many men understand how to fish "big water." There being so many small streams in this country, these are the waters that receive most of the attention of the local anglers. In addition, "big-water" fishing is an uncertain thing. You are just as apt as not to spend a fishless day on a big stream and little can be done about it. For the man who has only a few days for fishing, the small stream is a safer bet. Thus, I had plenty of elbow room.

A set-up of this sort is ideal for the purposes of the Solunar Theory. For observations to be of any value, they must be made of undisturbed fish. Day after day the placid waters of the big pools on the Loyalsock were untouched by intruders. Such is the perversity of human nature that I found myself resenting the very sight of another fisherman, instead of being grateful for the God-given solitude that I enjoyed most of the time.

I learned a lot about the river, the fish, the insect life and the Solunar Theory that spring and summer. As I had suspected, the timing of my schedule was decidedly behind the true schedule of aquatic activity. I soon learned to adapt it to actual conditions, however, so that I had an absolute check for future reference. On my return each evening, I entered in my diary a careful record of the day's experiences. That record is valuable. Also, it is the first contiguous record I had had the opportunity to assemble.

Angling is a contemplative sport. Spending as much time as I did in watching the behavior and movements of fish, it is not strange that while doing so I found ample time to consider and digest my findings. Having made serious mistakes in the past, I checked and rechecked my observations, so that, before the season came to a close, I felt certain that my findings were correct. It is unfortunate that never before had I found the opportunity to do any intensive and uninterrupted work on the activity schedule, but from the foregoing, you can see that it was out of the question.

With the various changes in the Solunar Theory since its inception; miscalculations and revised methods of computing the Solunar schedule, with the resultant inaccuracies, it may seem strange that any credence is placed in it at this time by anybody. On second thought, however, the reason is obvious. In the first place, the average Solunar period is about an hour and a half or two hours in duration. That fact in itself leaves a certain amount of latitude for miscalculation. Then, too, adverse temperatures, unsettled barometric conditions, low water, high water and many other factors all have their effects upon the timing of the schedule. On an ideal day, the fish respond early and continue their activity for as much as three and a half hours. With unfavorable conditions, the activity period may be confined to a sharp flurry of feeding, lasting only twenty minutes. It is an extremely variable thing; one that cannot be pinned down to a set schedule of absolute minutes.

Thus the times shown in the Solunar Tables can be regarded merely as averages at best. Not since the first year of their publication have my mistakes made a difference of more than an hour. This much difference in the time of arrival may be and frequently is offset by a variation of weather conditions from one day to the next.

Considering these things, the schedule has at no time been at *radical* difference with the true activity cycle. Meanwhile, those anglers who have had the breadth of vision to follow the schedule, have found that it is a guide to the best fishing of each day, and the quality of their sport has improved in spite of the fact that the whole thing was, and still is, in the process of experimentation.

When one takes into consideration the offsetting effects of adverse conditions upon the true schedule of activity periods, it can be seen quite readily just why it is impractical to trust too much in the observations of others. All too often do they fail to take into account *all* of the conditions that exist from day to day. Lacking the knowledge to do this, information received from them not only is useless—too often it is extremely misleading. About the only fellow I can trust completely with this job is my son Dick. Having grown up in the very atmosphere of the Solunar Theory, he knows the whole game and I can believe what he tells me. It seems too bad that more intelligent and uninterrupted research work cannot be done on the full solution of the problem, but that takes both time and money—and I have a living to earn. So I guess that it must be worked out on a gradual, year-to-year basis. At least, we are gaining on it annually.

As research progresses, I find that the "moon-up-moon-down" method of the old Southern market hunters comes close to hitting the mark only part of the time. "Moon up and moon down" does not tell the whole story by any means. With the exception of a few days, this method does not conform to the true schedule. And the fact that there is a shorter, but equally well defined, feeding period midway between the two main feeding periods seems to have escaped those old fellows completely.

In addition, I can find no evidence that they had any knowledge of "physical lag" in the effects of the Solunar influence on creatures of different degrees of development. They just adopted a method of loose approximation and applied it to *all creatures alike*. Taking all these things into consideration, perhaps it is just as well that I decided to hew out my own trail. The going has been difficult in spots, but we have learned a lot through the actual surmounting of difficulties.

I feel sure that about as close as we are going to be able to get to the absolute schedule through the trial-

and-error method is the way the schedule is being calculated at present. At the times of full moon and dark of the moon, the moon and the sun are functioning in unison, they, at those times, being approximately "in line." That being the case, the resultant of the directions of pull of the two heavenly bodies comes pretty close to being the true Solunar period. As the month progresses, the directions of pull of the moon and of the sun move farther apart each day so that, at the times of first quarter and third quarter, they are approximately at right angles to each other. At these times, the moon can be considered to be the complete control. These are the times when the "moon-up-moon-down" system seems to be the correct method of timing. In setting up the schedule, these four times of the month are used as key points. Just at what time of the month the sun ceases to act in conjunction with the moon and just at what point the moon becomes the full control, I cannot say with any authority. This much I do know. By averaging in the times of the Solunar periods between these four key points, so that the progression from day to day is smooth, the resultant schedule comes about as close to the true schedule as it is possible to come without knowing the absolute cause. When and if the actual cause of these activity periods is known *definitely*, so that it can be isolated, measured and timed, then the Solunar Theory can be reduced to the enviable status of an absolute science. It can be simplified to the point where two and two equal four. When that time comes, I have no doubt that these pages will make pretty funny reading. Until that time *does* come, these same pages will guide you to a lot more good fishing and good shooting than you ever can find just by trusting to luck.

Many times I have been asked if I can account for the existence of the "minor" feeding periods that occur midway between the two "major" periods. I am sorry to say that I cannot. I can conjecture, but anybody's guess is as good as mine. When the moon is in the first-quarter or the third-quarter position, the pull of the sun is at right angles to the pull of the moon. That would surely establish the "minor" period for those two days and, possibly, for one or two days before and after them, making a possible total of ten days of each month. What about the remaining days of each lunar period? Why does the "minor" feeding period continue to manifest itself on those days, midway between the "major" periods? It may be that *habit*, created by stimulated feeding on those ten days, carries through until the actual stimulus once more establishes these "minor" periods. The fact remains that there they are and that wild life responds to them, often emphatically. The true answer will have to wait until we find out more of the actual cause of the entire activity cycle. Until then, take my word for it and keep them in mind. You will have better fishing if you do.

So much for the Solunar Theory, as a theory; its history and its gradual, labored formation. Working from effect back to cause is apt to be a slow job. Surely it is in this case, where the cause is so well hidden and, at present at least, so intangible and indefinite. It might be more interesting to take a look at the manner in which the stimulus of Solunar influence affects the various classes of living creatures. You don't have to be a fisherman to have the Solunar Theory play a fairly important part in your life.

CHAPTER SIX

As EXPLAINED previously, aquatic insects seem to react promptly and characteristically to the urge of a Solunar period. In the matter of "hatches," a term with which every trout fisherman is familiar, this reaction is often quite noticeable. Here, as in most cases, there are other factors that play an important part. We know that temperatures constitute a vital factor in the development of insect hatches. For those who may be unfamiliar with the term, a "hatch" is that time at which the members of a certain group or family of stream-bottom larvæ cut loose from the bottom stones and rise to the surface, where they break their cases and emerge as winged insects or duns. If temperatures are unfavorable—too cold or, for that matter, too hot—the hatch will be retarded and, in some cases, completely stopped. If weather conditions are unfavorable—rain, storms and the like—again the progress of the hatch may be retarded. But if other conditions are favorable, then the big hatches—those times when the air is filled with thousands upon thousands of ephemera—these huge hatches, more often than not, occur concurrently with the major Solunar periods.

Aquatic insects that hatch nocturnally (and there are many of them) make their way to the rocks, trees and bushes along shore, there to emerge from their nymphal cases and await the auspicious time to fly from the sheltering foliage and engage in their nuptial dance over the stream. Here again the effects of a Solunar period are quite evident in the determination of the time for the nuptial flight, providing, of course, that there is no offsetting factor. This does not mean that there will be no hatches at other times, when Solunar periods are not in progress. Far from it. But, under equal conditions, the intensity of the hatch seems to be governed by its proximity to a major Solunar period.

Cicadas, often called the "seventeen-year locusts," make their presence known on hot summer days by giving vent to their "song" from their perches high in the trees. Usually this song is most prevalent during the hottest midday hours of our summer days. Yet, not once but many times, have I heard the song of these insects on summer evenings *after dark* while a major Solunar period has been in progress.

There is an evident increase in honey-gathering activity among the bees during Solunar periods. Between times, a good share of a colony will fuss around the hive, but the arrival of a Solunar period will put them to work in real earnest.

Fish furnish perhaps the most satisfactory proving ground for the observation of the effects of Solunar influence. It was because of fish that the experiments were first begun, and for that reason most of my time has been spent in the observation and study of the effects of Solunar influence on them. I suppose that I have seen literally thousands of Solunar periods "come in" while I have been on lake or stream. As might be expected, there have been some unusual and interesting reactions. There is neither time, space nor necessity to recount many of them here. But there are a few happenings that will serve to illustrate how completely the cycle of feeding periods and rest periods influence not only the habits but the very existence of all fish.

Some years ago, as an educational measure, the Pennsylvania Board of Fish Commissioners took over a section of Spring Creek near Bellefonte, Pennsylvania. They fenced in the area they wished to control, gave this section of stream an elaborate manicure of stream improvement to provide the last word in furnished homes for the trout, and proceeded to stock the stream heavily with large fish. The grounds were landscaped, gravel walks and liberal parking spaces were built, a "club house" was erected and every measure was taken to make things pleasant for the fishermen of the state. They named this project the Fishermen's Paradise. Any holder of a Pennsylvania fishing license is entitled to come there and fish, not more than five times a season and subject to the rules laid down by the Commission.

About two years after its completion, they were kind enough to invite me to speak at the dinner that is held each year on the evening before the annual grand opening of the Paradise. As might be expected, I talked about the Solunar Theory. I explained what it is, how it works and extolled its advantages. They listened attentively.

The next day dawned cold, foggy, with now and then a spit of rain. It was the sort of day that calls for wet-fly fishing with the fly fished as close to the stream bottom as possible. Anglers had been lined up outside the gates of the Paradise since well before dawn and, by the time the eight-o'clock signal sounded, there were several thousand fishermen distributed along the banks of the stream.

At the eight-o'clock signal, every one of the fishermen present cast his fly into the heavily stocked waters. About half of them hooked trout—big trout—immediately and the commotion kicked up while those fish were being landed or lost fairly lashed the waters of the little trout stream into a lather.

The Solunar period that day was scheduled to arrive at about eleven o'clock. Between eight and eleven the section of Spring Creek that lies within the boundaries of the paradise was literally hammered flat by the earnest and continuous casting of the fly fishermen standing almost shoulder to shoulder on its banks. It seemed to be expected of me that I should fish, especially during the Solunar Period. I looked at the disturbed water, the crowds and the weather and my heart sank. Then, too, I could not overlook the fact that these were hatchery-reared trout, recently stocked and not yet accustomed to their new environment. In the hatchery they had been fed at approximately the same time each day, regardless of Solunar periods, and I wondered if these hatchery fish had been in natural surroundings long enough to have learned to respond to Solunar periods. The outlook seemed pretty hopeless.

At ten-thirty, although a light, misty rain was falling and the air was cold, I went to my car and set up a fly rod. Having removed the barbs from half a dozen flies (to comply with regulations), I tried to find a spot on the bank where there would be room to cast. After some searching, I located a place where the crowd was not too thick. It wasn't a choice location by any means, but at least I had elbow room.

Instead of fishing, I stood on the bank and watched the water. All seemed to be quiet and the man next to me grumbled to himself about the fishing being, as he termed it, "lousy." Then, out of the corner of my eye, I thought I detected a movement under the surface. I watched more carefully. Sure enough, the slow, confident roll of a feeding trout. It was a long cast but I thought I might reach him. As I unlimbered my tackle, another trout rolled under the surface. Then another and another. Contrary to my expectations, the fish actually were responding to the Solunar period and going on the feed.

On my second cast I hooked a trout. I played him halfway to the bank before lowering my rod so that he could shake the barbless fly from his mouth. But that was just the start. During the next twenty minutes I hooked and released ten more large fish. After the second or third, a crowd began to gather. Three of them walked into my back cast and were hooked, not seriously as luck would have it. After twenty minutes, I had had my fill of exhibition fishing. Eleven trout and three fishermen in twenty minutes—a record that will stand for some time at the Paradise.

Eleven trout in twenty minutes is not at all unusual if the trout are feeding. The remarkable aspect of this affair is that hatchery-reared trout, freshly stocked, should respond so completely to the feeding urge of a Solunar period, even under the worst imaginable conditions of bad weather and disturbed water. Since then the Pennsylvania Fish Commission secures a supply of Solunar Tables each year.

During the second year of publication of the Solunar Tables, George Greenfield, at that time rod-and-gun editor of *The New York Times*, decided to conduct a test to find out for himself—and his readers—if the Solunar Theory were all it should be. Accordingly, he arranged to receive reports of a week-end's fishing from men who planned to fish the trout streams of Pennsylvania, New York, New Jersey and Connecticut. Each one of these men was asked to keep track of the time during which he experienced the best fishing on that particular Saturday.

The following Monday Greenfield published his findings in his column. In all of the four states named, his spotters had found the trout to be most active at approximately the same time on the preceding Saturday afternoon—right during the major Solunar period.

The response of trout to the urge of a Solunar period can be, and often is, a tricky and deceptive thing, particularly to the eye of the untrained observer. Generally speaking, trout will feed when there is a supply of food present. When a hatch of insects comes on the water, the fish usually respond with a flurry of feeding that lasts as long as the insects are drifting, regardless of Solunar periods. This is not always the case, but it happens often. The effects of Solunar influence in cases of this kind evidence themselves in the *behavior* of the fish at the time. When trout are feeding to a "between-period" hatch, the character of the rise is quite typical. Instead of taking up convenient feeding stations in the current, just under the line of drift of the insects floating on the surface, the fish are more apt to feed from their resting stations on the stream bottom. They rise sporadically, with a characteristic, hurried strike, and the haste with which they take their food shows clearly that they are apprehensive of showing themselves to their many natural enemies. It is at these times that the fish become what anglers call "selective." They will feed on one particular type of fly and ignore all other forms of food. Artificial flies, in order to interest them during the course of such a "selective rise," must bear as close a resemblance to the natural insect as it is possible to make them. Fishing during a "selective rise" is more apt than not to be an exasperating bit of business.

Many times a "between-periods" hatch will be allowed to drift away untouched by the trout. But, in fifteen years of careful observation, *I have never seen a hatch of insects ignored if it matures during a major Solunar period.*

During a Solunar period, the behavior of the trout is quite different from what it is at other times. They seem to lose much of their natural caution and evidently have no fear of exposing themselves. Instead of feeding from their resting stations, they move to feeding positions in the current, frequently in clear view, and they take their food with the "tip-up" rise that consists merely of elevating the head to the surface and sucking in the flies with the minimum of effort. Rarely are they at all selective at these times and they are prone to sample almost any type of food, be it natural or artificial.

Every fisherman knows that the regular daily feeding periods, particularly of fresh-water fish, are at dawn and dusk. These two times of day generally represent the high spots of the average fishing day. Not infrequently, however, the fish will fail completely at these times to respond to the most tempting offerings of the angler's art. Should the glass be falling, the trout will be unresponsive, regardless of the fact that it is evening and that they generally feed at that time.

One of the more common causes of failure to indulge in the "evening rise" is one that is not taken into consideration by the majority of fishermen. When a Solunar period has occurred just prior to the normal evening feeding period, almost always the fish will have had their supper early and their activity will be at an end by the time dusk arrives. I have seen this happen literally countless times. Yet, where water conditions are anywhere near normal, I have never seen the fish fail to "go on the feed" when the evening feeding period and a major Solunar period arrive concurrently.

Bass, both the large-mouth and small-mouth variety, respond to Solunar periods in great shape. In Chapter One, I have already told you of my experience on Lake

Moon Up - Moon Down 65

Helenblazes, Florida. That same type of thing I have duplicated hundreds of times. I don't think that I ever will bring out as large a catch as we did that day, but, in numbers and general activity, the experience was not unusual.

As a matter of fact, I know of no variety of fish that does not respond to Solunar periods. Certainly saltwater fish feed according to the Solunar schedule.

In 1938 I had the pleasure of being the guest of the Nova Scotia government at the International Tuna Tournament at Liverpool, Nova Scotia. The first day of the tournament, I rode as an observer in the boat of Tom Wheeler, one of the four British contestants. From dawn until eight o'clock in the morning of the first day of the tournament, a time of day when one would expect the fishing to be good, there was little activity. One of the Cuban team hooked a huge shark near one of the herring nets but, aside from that, there was nothing to disturb the tranquillity of the bay.

The Solunar period was scheduled for eight-thirty and I watched the water about the mouth of the bay with interest. Sure enough, right on schedule, I saw the surface broken by the dorsal fin of a feeding tuna. Then came a second and a third and, within fifteen minutes, the bay was fairly alive with huge feeding tuna, slashing through the schools of herring.

For three days I checked carefully the times at which tuna were hooked by the various members of the three competing teams of Cuba, Great Britain and the United States. With one exception, every fish was hooked during a Solunar period. That exception was foul-hooked through the dorsal fin by the late Paul Townsend, captain of the United States team.

Sebastian Inlet, Florida, is, perhaps, one of the finest places to observe the workings of the Solunar Theory. This inlet is an artificial one, created by the government so that ocean fish can have access to the quieter waters of Indian and Banana Rivers. Along this part of the coast, the high-water interval (H. W. I.) is such that low tide approximately coincides with the major Solunar periods.

With the exception of a mild flurry of feeding at the high-tide point (the minor Solunar period) the inlet flows like a raceway, empty of fish for at least eighteen hours of the twenty-four. As the feeding period approaches, however, schools of mullet appear in the shallows. Careful watch of the breakers out on the bar often will detect game fish—big ones—outlined in the transparent tops of the waves as they curl up to crash over the bar. Then, and only then, the fishing in the inlet is beyond belief. It is difficult to cast a lure of any description into those racing waters without having a fish strike it savagely.

This activity continues for an hour or more. The commercial fishermen ply their trade with homemade rods and lures, stout lines and heavy reels. At the close of the feeding period, the activity tapers off. Fewer and fewer fish are caught. The commercial men reel in their lines, start up their motors and sail their catches across the river to the little fish houses that dot the shore.

Experience has taught them that they will have ten hours in which to clean and ice their fish, tend to their tackle and kill time until the next active feeding period arrives.

As with other creatures, the effect of Solunar influence is not always evident with individual fish. Where there is a school of fish, however, the increase in activity is nearly always clear. There seems to be a group reaction, wherein the increased activity on the part of the more susceptible members is transmitted or infused among the remainder of the school.

Another characteristic effect of Solunar influence on fish is the marked tendency to "surface" during Solunar periods. Even goldfish in a bowl on your library table will rise to the surface and swim about, blowing bubbles, during Solunar periods. Bass leave the deep water and cruise about in the shallows. Fish seem to lose their natural caution and have no objection to exposing themselves to view at these times. Anglers find that surface lures are usually more effective than the underwater varieties during Solunar periods.

Already the Solunar Theory is developing its commercial uses. I have been reliably informed, by a man who is in a position to know, that many of the commercial fisheries off the New Jersey coast schedule their dory launchings according to the Solunar Tables. They have found that they make better catches that way. A man who breeds and raises tropical fish, for sale to the pet shops of New York City, makes it a point to feed his tiny charges during Solunar periods. He has learned that by so doing more of the food is consumed and less is allowed to accumulate on the bottoms of the tanks. His fish grow faster and he has to clean the tanks less frequently. Party-boat captains, operating from ports along the New Jersey and Long Island coasts, and some of the Florida "Gulf-stream" captains, find that they get better results and their patrons get better fishing if each day is planned according to the Solunar schedule. By being on the fishing grounds during Solunar periods and spending the intervening time with sailing and meals, the best of each day's sport is made available for the fishermen who ride their boats.

For my own part, my copy of the Solunar Tables is just as much a standard item of equipment in my fishing kit as are my fly rods or my reels. Having planned my fishing days by them for fifteen years, I know I can depend on them to keep me from missing the best that each day has to offer.

Activity among aquatic life is not confined to fish and insects alone. Salt-water crabs respond to a Solunar period just as enthusiastically as any of the other aquatic creatures. When we lived in Florida, now and then we would go crabbing on the shoals of Daytona Beach near Mosquito Inlet. Between Solunar periods, the sand flats would be almost deserted, with only an odd crab now and then, buried up to his eyes in the sand. As the Solunar periods came in, the crabs would leave the deep waters of the inlet and come up on the flats to feed—big, blue fellows that certainly made fine eating. Armed with long-handled nets and burlap bags, we had no trouble, during the first half-hour or so of the activity period, capturing all we could use.

Only recently it has been brought to my attention that oysters, packed in barrels for shipment, open their shells and "smack their lips" when the Solunar periods arrive. The noise is clearly audible and they make quite a fuss. Scientists, to the attention of whom I have brought this reaction, attribute it to "habit behavior" rather than to the response to any definite stimulus. Unfortunately, oysters kept in captivity live for only a few weeks, so that the cause of their behavior is still subject to argument. Some day I hope to settle the matter by conducting observations over the period of a *conclusive* space of time with clams, oysters and mussels in the controlled waters of a tidal pool where they will live in their natural environment. Then we shall see.

CHAPTER SEVEN

It IS an absorbing study to observe the effects of Solunar influence on birds. Not all of them respond alike and care should be exercised in forming conclusions. Nevertheless, the effects do manifest themselves and the careful observer will have no difficulty in spotting them.

When I resigned from the bank, my first thought was to bring my health back to normal if possible. The doctors prescribed rest—rest in large doses. Thus, a good share of that summer was spent in a steamer chair on the screened veranda of our house in Orange. From this vantage point, I could both see and hear what went on in the large lot that lay directly behind our house.

It was not difficult to know when a Solunar period was in progress. The whistle of a quail and the familiar "ka-woo, whoo, whoo" of the ring-necked dove would be all but drowned out by the music of hundreds of songbirds. Many times Beth would come to the porch and say,

"You don't need a trout stream to check up on your Solunar Tables. Just listen to the birds, singing their little heads off."

This bird song was always accompanied by a great amount of fluttering and flying about. Our lawn would be covered with feeding birds and now and then a rabbit or two would come over and sample our garden.

One winter we set up a feeding shelf outside our dining-room window. It was interesting to note the manner in which this shelf was patronized. If food should be put out first thing in the morning, it was all gone within the hour. That was to be expected. Early morning is a normal, daily feeding period with birds just as it is with fish. On the other hand, if we allowed the shelf to remain empty until the morning was well advanced, then the food stayed there, untouched, until the next Solunar period arrived. Very seldom did a Solunar period pass without having the shelf picked clean of every crumb.

In several letters from users of the Solunar Tables, mention has been made of the coincidence of bird activity and the Solunar periods. The writers have discovered that the birds show up on schedule as I had said they would. One man in Baltimore writes:

"It's a mighty nice thing to be able to announce to dinner guests that at 2:30 that Sunday afternoon seven pairs of cardinals would be on the feeding shelf and then to have them *be* there—all fourteen of them—at the specified time."

Every salt-water fisherman will tell you that the sea gulls are a tremendous aid in helping them to find the schools of feeding fish. I often wonder if it has occurred to any of these men to wonder how the gulls happen to know when the schools will be active in deep water several miles offshore. Every one who has spent much time at the seashore knows the familiar sight of flocks of sea gulls, sitting on the rocks, sandspits and pilings, preening their feathers or dozing in the sun, evidently with never a thought of food. Some day, just for the fun of it, watch a colony of resting gulls *when a Solunar period is scheduled to arrive.* For no reason evident to the observer, the birds will take off in small groups of two, three, five or ten and head for the open sea. Almost before you realize it, the shore, where hundreds of gulls had been but a few minutes before, will be completely deserted. Nature, Solunar influence—call it what you like—tells them that the feeding period has arrived and that the predatory fish will be slashing through the schools of menhaden, herring and mullet offshore. That means food for the gulls and they clean up the bits of fish drifting on the surface while they follow the daily slaughter.

Some of the waterfowl hunters are learning that the Solunar Tables are helpful in planning a day's duck shooting. To be sure, the best times to shoot duck, day in and day out, are early morning and late evening. The present-day four-o'clock rule precludes any shooting during the evening flight. Nevertheless, these two times of day mark the extremes of activity among the ducks.

Unless you happen to have a good point-shooting blind, these two flights often are not very productive, particularly if the weather is clear and the ducks are flying high. They do not decoy as readily then as they do during the day. It is when you find the ducks trading restlessly back and forth all day that you are apt to find the most productive shooting.

Moon Up - Moon Down

As a general rule, even though it happens to be a "bluebird" day, there is a certain amount of activity among the ducks during a Solunar period. Small bunches will break off from the "ricks" that are resting in deep water and these decoy readily during Solunar periods. Like all wild life, ducks seem to lose much of their sense of caution during the activity periods and they will come to your decoys more readily and less critically than at other times. Knowing this in advance, the day can be planned so that the activity periods shall not be missed.

Ring-necked pheasants have an unpleasant habit of spending a good share of their time in the swamps, briar patches and thick cover of the lowlands. To hunt them in these difficult places is a tiresome and heartbreaking piece of business. During Solunar periods, however, the birds leave the swamps and the heavy cover and move to higher ground in search of food. Then they are easy to find; they will "lie for the dog," instead of running, and furnish excellent shooting. For several seasons I checked the habits of pheasants before, during and after Solunar periods. It is seldom that they do not follow the Solunar schedule. Even though the upland cover may have been hunted just prior to a Solunar period, the birds will leave the protection of the swamps and head for higher ground as soon as the feeding period arrives.

During the fall of 1941, grouse hunters throughout this section of central Pennsylvania did a lot of complaining about the low level to which our grouse shooting had fallen. That spring had shown us an excellent nesting season. One game warden told me that he had seen a hen grouse with a brood of fourteen chicks. I saw two broods of eight chicks each and others reported an abundance of birds. We had high hopes for the fall shooting.

When September rolled around, disturbing reports began to come in. The annual grouse field trials had difficulty in locating enough birds to enable the dogs to show their worth. Men who live on the outskirts of the "Black Forest"—that vast wilderness of second-growth timber that lies to the Northwest of Williamsport—reported a decided scarcity of birds. Famous concentration points—covers that have yielded thousands upon thousands of grouse in past years—proved to be nearly deserted. With the nesting season that we had had and the large number of birds reported in the spring months, the scarcity in the fall didn't make any sense. The birds *must* be there, somewhere.

After walking countless miles through the big woods and finding comparatively few birds, my son and I held a conference. It has always been my contention that the old-time grouse hunters of Pennsylvania actually know very little about grouse hunting. True, they are, for the most part, excellent shots, but they learned their grouse shooting when it was not uncommon to flush seventy-five and a hundred grouse in a single day. Now that the birds are not so plentiful, these same old-timers have trouble finding any game at all. My son and I decided to discard what we had learned of the Black

Forest and other "deep-woods" shooting and do a bit of private research.

Because of the size of our deer herd, and also the present height of our second-growth timber, the natural food in the deep woods is scarce. Grouse, in order to live, have had to find their food elsewhere. Thus they have taken to the woodlots, the clearings and, frequently, to the open fields. Aspen and alder thickets, formerly associated only with woodcock, now hold grouse in surprising abundance. Reasoning that the birds had left the deep woods, we hunted the woodlots of the semi-open farm lands in the rolling hills of this vicinity. We began to turn up more birds than formerly.

One day, on one of our woodlot tours, we chanced upon a promising-looking spot. Rolling hills with open fields and bushy hedge rows, with a woodlot—part hemlock and part hardwood—that lay in a fold in the hills. We parked the car, obtained permission to hunt from the farmer and set out. It was fairly late in the afternoon and we had only a little more than an hour before the five-o'clock deadline. We hunted through the hemlock grove first—no birds. Then, at the top of the hill, we found a clearing, strewn with piles of lopped-off branches ("slashing" is the term for it in these parts). As we entered the clearing, a grouse flushed out of range, then another and another. In all, we put twelve birds out of that clearing, all of them out of range and wilder than hawks.

Two days later, two friends of mine came up from Baltimore to hunt with me. Thus my son was left to his own devices for his day out of school. While we shot some coveys that had been located earlier in the year, my boy, Dick, took one of his friends to the woodlot we had found. Our party of four guns, with two good dogs and not less than sixteen miles of hard going behind us, showed up that evening having flushed twenty birds during the day. Dick and his friend hunted not quite two hours, without a dog, and flushed thirty-five birds right in "our" woodlot that is not more than a mile in extent by the longest possible measurement.

A few days later, Dick and I visited the woodlot again. Our high hopes for top-notch shooting, with plenty of birds, were soon blasted. Search as we would, we found only three birds and these so wild that we could get nowhere near them. We returned home, birdless and a little puzzled.

It so happened that neither of us had found the opportunity to hunt this woodlot during a Solunar period. I had been unusually busy at my desk and the boy had been, for the most part, occupied in school.

The day before the season closed, Dick burst into my office, his eyes shining with excitement.

"Dad," he shouted, "guess what happened. Bill and a friend of his went over to our woodlot yesterday. Now you know how those fellows shoot. They both came back with their limits of birds and Bill told me that they could have killed as many more without any trouble. He said the birds weren't wild and wouldn't flush until they had almost stepped on them. They put up nearly fifty in less than three hours."

I thought this over for a minute.

"What time of day were they there?" I asked him.

"Yesterday afternoon, from two until about four-thirty."

I picked up a copy of the Solunar Tables from my desk and looked up the day under discussion.

"There's the answer," I told him. "Those two fellows hunted right through a major Solunar period. The birds were in the hardwood and the clearing, feeding and unwilling to leave the feeding cover. That's why they didn't flush until they were almost kicked out."

We looked at each other and smiled with mutual understanding.

"I wonder," said Dick, "when you're going to learn how to use your own Solunar Tables."

This experience is not by any means an isolated instance. Many times I have hunted covers that I know hold plenty of grouse, only to find an odd bird or two. Later I have returned to that cover during a feeding period to find all the grouse a man could wish for.

The ruffed grouse of our Pennsylvania woods is, perhaps, the wildest, smartest and most cautious of all of our game birds, even including our wild turkey. Yet, smart as he is, he seems to lose a great share of his natural caution during a Solunar period. Without question, you can get much closer to him during Solunar periods than at other times. In this, he is not unusual, as the same holds true of all of the wild creatures—at least, all of which I have any first-hand knowledge. Between Solunar periods, grouse will usually be in the safe cover of the hemlock groves or, on occasion, dusting themselves in sunny clearings. Then it is difficult, if not next to impossible, to get within gunshot of them. During Solunar periods, however, when they are in their feeding cover, they will lie close for the dog and furnish wing shooting that you will never forget.

Quail seem to govern their daily feeding habits according to the Solunar cycle. Like pheasants, they spend a good share of their time in or near the protection of tangled swamp growth, briar patches or those well-nigh impenetrable jungles that are known in Florida as "bay heads." There they are safe from most of their natural enemies and they quickly take cover when danger threatens.

During Solunar periods, however, these little game birds move into the feed patches and the open fields. There they will lie close for the dog and are readily found. Upland cover that is "used" by a known number of coveys often will be completely empty of birds, while at other times birds will be plentiful.

In the winter of 1941, my son and I hunted quail and dove in the lowlands of South Carolina. We were guests at one of the large plantations in the vicinity of Charleston and had ten thousand acres of good cover at our disposal.

While our host uses the plantation only as a winter home, the multitudinous details of its management are, in effect, of the same importance and volume as though he were conducting a small, private business venture. Consequently, each morning found him at his desk while Dick and I busied ourselves in one or another of his several dove fields, where we joyfully fired an abundance of ammunition, the result of which was a tremendous commotion with relatively little damage.

The afternoons were spent in quail shooting, or, to be more explicit, quail hunting. Our host is bountifully supplied with dogs and those which we used are all field-trial champions—the finest of the breed. A quail hunt at the plantation was nothing short of a five-alarm fire. A station wagon carried two brace of dogs, in suitable wire cages, together with sundry dog tack and a few members of the party. Another car carried the plantation superintendent, the dog handler and such other dogs as might be brought along. At an appointed spot, the head hostler and one of his assistants awaited the party with horses equipped with saddles, saddle holsters for the guns, saddlebags, etc. The whole affair was quite impressive, all in the best tradition, and needful of not a little staff work.

At the time of our visit, it so happened that the major Solunar periods arrived during the mornings, so that, by the time our *entourage* reached the cover chosen for that day, the quail already had fed and retired to the safety of the briar patches and overgrown thickets among the live oaks. In four of these excursions, using experienced dogs of proven ability, we managed to turn up exactly three covies of quail—this, mind you, in covers that were used by not less than twenty-five or thirty coveys, to the definite knowledge of the men who spent their days in those very covers.

It pays to consult the Solunar Tables before going quail hunting.

I spoke of this to my host but he would have none of the suggestion. In the first place, plantation routine should not be disrupted. In the second place, my contention was not scientifically proven and may or may not be true. So we covered miles of unproductive territory which, two or three hours earlier, could and probably would have furnished excellent shooting.

Offsetting our experience was that of the dog handler who made it his daily routine to train the younger dogs each morning. Youngsters in the field require close attention and frequent correction. To attempt to train them from horseback only complicates matters. On foot, the handler can reach them more quickly and correct their mistakes at the time of their happening. This same dog handler, who accompanied us on our afternoon hunts, found, on foot, from four to six coveys of birds each morning of our stay at the plantation. While my contention that quail are more easily found during Solunar periods may not be scientifically proven, it stands to reason that where there is that much smoke there is bound to be a little fire.

Meanwhile, Dick and I put the Solunar periods to good use in the dove fields. When the dove are not disposed to feed, no amount of shooing about, on the part of Negroes hired for the purpose, will drive the birds into the feeding fields. They merely fly around among the trees and ignore their man-made cafeterias. When, however, a feeding period is in progress, a minor matter such as shooting and general commotion will not keep them out of the feeding fields. I asked one of the Negroes if the fuss we made wouldn't keep the birds away. His reply was enlightening.

"Noh suh," he answered. "When a dove want to fly, he fly. Don't make no diffunce wheah you is."

And that about sums it up. When a Solunar period is in progress and a dove makes up his mind to feed, feed he will, come hell or high water. Chase him out of one field and he will fly to another. But when the feeding period is ended and he has filled his crop, you may as well unload your gun and go home. Your dove shooting is over until the next feeding period arrives.

Confirming my observation of the effect of Solunar influence on birds are many letters in my files from users of the Solunar Tables. These include reports of owners of feeding shelves, dog trainers (who must, of necessity, find birds in order to work their dogs), hunters and amateur naturalists. Unfortunately, little has been done, at least to my knowledge, in observing the effects of Solunar periods on the behavior of migratory birds, insofar as actual migration flights are concerned. I suppose that will have to come later, time and facilities permitting. No contiguous, day-by-day record of bird activity has been made by me. But the hundreds, yes thousands, of unrelated observations that have been made, not only by myself but by the many individuals who write to me of their findings, cannot help but point in the right direction. It is not my contention that the Solunar Theory is "scientifically" proven in its relation to birds. However, the coincidence of bird activity and Solunar periods is entirely too common to be disregarded. Knowing that these things *do* happen with regularity, it seems short-sighted not to put this knowledge to good use when opportunity presents itself.

CHAPTER EIGHT

REPTILES respond to Solunar periods, much the same as other creatures. On a sunny day, turtles climb up on floating logs to sun themselves, but they are back in the water again when a Solunar period arrives, answering the promptings of nature in their search for food.

The owner of a large collection of snakes puts the Solunar Tables to good use in the care of her pets. One of the problems in maintaining a collection of caged reptiles is that of feeding. A caged snake is lethargic at best and it takes its food infrequently and reluctantly. By placing food—usually live birds, mice, rats or insects—in the cages at the beginning of a major Solunar period, the owner of the collection has found that the snakes feed more readily and stay in better physical condition than if they are fed more or less at random.

Animals respond to Solunar influence variously, according to the habits of the animal and its degree of development. Mice and rats, although nocturnal feeders for the most part, respond to Solunar periods during the daylight hours as well as at night. In our house in Orange the openings in the cellar all had been screened with heavy wire as a preventive measure. One spring, a family of rats took up their abode under our side porch. The entrance to their warren was only a few feet from the garbage can. Although this can was equipped with a heavy metal cover, the rats remained optimistic and showed profound interest in the can and its contents, even though they were unable to avail themselves of its luxuries. Because of the screening, I knew that they could not find their way into the cellar, so I said nothing about them to Beth. Unfortunately, she discovered our visitors before they had been there a week. She was all out for immediate extermination but I persuaded her to hold off for a while, to the delight of my big setter Bill, who fairly haunted the entrance to their home. His first duty each day was to poke his nose under the porch as far as possible, sniff his lungs full of delectable rat smells and then blow huge gusts of sniffed-in air back at the rats.

I had an excellent view of their passageway and of the garbage can by concealing myself behind the curtains of our kitchen window. Against Beth's wishes, I would often place choice tidbits just outside their front door, first making sure that this food was made available only *between* Solunar periods. Now and then the food would disappear soon after it was placed there. It may have been taken by one of the many neighborhood dogs that called every day to romp with Bill or it may have been taken by the rats. More often, however, it would stay where I had placed it until the arrival of a Solunar period, remaining there sometimes as long as an hour or two. Never did a Solunar period come to a close with any of the food uneaten.

In common with all of the creatures that I have

observed, these rats seemed to lose a good share of their caution during Solunar periods. It was not unusual to see two or three of them investigating the possibilities of the garbage can at these times, but not once, in the entire month that I watched them, did I so much as catch a glimpse of a rat unless a Solunar period was in progress. After a month of rat observation, they displayed the bad judgment to raise a family of youngsters and the worse luck to have Beth spot one or two of the little ones from the kitchen window. The investigation of rats and their habits came to a sudden and catastrophic close that same day despite my protests. She would stand just so much but there were limits.

A friend of mine in Philadelphia, who is an engineer and scientifically minded, became involved in bossing the job of reallocating the machinery in the plant where he was employed. It was necessary to do this work slowly and at night because the machines were used in the manufacture of woolen goods in the daytime and had to be in running order each morning. The building, an old wooden structure, had its quota of rats and mice, and my friend had plenty of time to check up on their activities.

He found that both the rats and the mice reacted to the Solunar periods, regardless of the noise of the work going on in the factory. The mice would come out of hiding at the beginning of the periods and, as a rule, would be in evidence for the full hour and a half or two hours. They seemed to lose most of their caution and ran about the floor quite boldly, only scooting for cover if they were disturbed by one of the workmen. The rats, on the other hand, were more reluctant to show themselves. Only after the feeding period had been in progress for some time would they emerge from their holes and then for not more than twenty minutes or so at most.

Wintertime is the best time to get clean-cut observations of animals, particularly if the weather be cold. During the severe weather, animals spend much of their time in their dens, warrens or burrows, where they can keep warm. Only when they are in search of food do they venture into the cold outdoors. Shortly after the Solunar Tables were first published, a man in Pennsylvania wrote me an interesting letter. He said that his house was several miles from his little boy's school. Thus, it was necessary for him to call at the school in his automobile several times each day to pick up the youngster. The school was surrounded by tall oak trees and the acorns attracted the squirrels in the neighborhood.

While waiting for the boy, this man noticed that sometimes the trees were alive with squirrels, while at other times there wouldn't be a squirrel in sight. Finally, out of curiosity, he checked the squirrel activity against the Solunar Tables and found that about the only time that he would see squirrels in any quantity would be during the major Solunar periods.

The following winter I contracted a bad case of "flu" and was confined to the house for almost a month. During the several weeks of convalescence, I had ample opportunity to investigate the effects of Solunar influence on a colony of squirrels that overran the two large oak trees on our lawn. My observations were the same as the other fellow's. During the major Solunar periods of that intensely cold January, our trees would be alive with squirrels for half an hour or an hour. Then they would disappear and no more would be seen of them until the next activity period arrived.

The same rule holds good for rabbits, foxes or any of the burrowing animals during the winter months. Between Solunar periods, they usually spend their time in the warm interiors of their warrens but, with the arrival of a Solunar period, they generally are out in the open in search of food.

Many times during the hunting season, I have found rabbits almost everywhere in certain feeding covers during a major Solunar period. Several days later, a search of the same covers between Solunar periods would reveal not a single rabbit. There are many letters in my files that support my own observations in this regard.

The larger animals also are apt to be on the move during Solunar periods. Deer, bear and so on are in evidence at these times because it is then that they move about in search of food. Bear, of course, hibernate in the winter months, but during the spring, summer and fall they are much in evidence during the activity periods. Even cows in a meadow show some indications of activity during Solunar periods. Although it is difficult to associate the word "activity" with cows in a meadow, there is, nevertheless, a noticeable difference in their behavior from time to time. For a while, I had occasion several times each week to drive by a "demonstration farm" of one of the large milk companies. In the field that bordered the road was a herd of about thirty thoroughbred Guernseys and I kept watch on their behavior whenever I passed the field. Between Solunar periods, most of the herd would be lying down in the shade or standing about, absorbed in rumination, as cows are apt to be. During Solunar periods, most of them would be grazing or moving about the field. In the months that I watched them, I did not see a single cow lying down during one of the activity periods. In observing cows, it seems to be more important to take note of what they do *not* do, as their movements are somewhat too leisurely to provide positive results in so far as activity is concerned.

Dogs provide interesting subjects for observation. While it is never wholly satisfactory to consider the movements of any *individual* creature of any class, dogs have certain characteristics that will show positive or negative results quite clearly. We have had three dogs and a puppy since the Solunar idea first came to light and the reactions of these four have been identical.

Our first one (after the birth of the Solunar Theory) was a little wire-haired fox terrier who adopted Beth and Dick one day when she was bringing the boy home from school. The day was bitterly cold and she and the youngster were hurrying home as fast as they could. Dick was the first to notice the little dog that trotted along behind them. An hour after they reached the house, the little beast was still shivering against our front door, so Beth brought him in and fed him some warm milk to thaw him out a bit. Knowing that he must be lost, she looked at his license tag and found that it had been issued in a town at least fifteen miles away. We notified the police and five days later the dog's owner showed up, found that Barney had picked out a good home and presented him to us.

At night, before turning in, we would let Barney out for his evening run. Usually he would be back, scratching at the door, within fifteen minutes. Two or three times each month, however, Barney would fail to show up. No amount of whistling or calling made any difference, so we would retire without him.

Our bedroom was at the rear of the house and Barney, instead of barking at the front door where nobody would hear him, would come and bark under my window, usually at about two in the morning. Not until he heard me moving about would he trot back to the front door and be waiting there for me. He knew he was wrong and acted very penitent when I scolded him, but he kept on making his midnight forays as long as he lived. At that time, I didn't know why he was so persistent about them but I found out later.

The next official Knight dog was a big English setter named Bill. Throughout his puppy years, Bill was turned out in his run in the evening, but when he arrived at the age of discretion we would let him out at the front door each night for his pre-bedtime jaunt. Like

Barney, Bill would disappear two or three times a month and we would find him curled up at the back door the next morning. With his heavy coat, weather didn't bother him in the least and his guilty conscience kept him from barking to wake us up. He was very guilty about his misbehavior but he did not mend his ways.

Beth and I were talking one night about the similarity of the behavior of the two dogs, so we checked over Bill's past indiscretions and compared the dates with the Solunar Tables. We found that when a major Solunar period was scheduled to arrive near midnight, that was the time when Bill would fail to show up until morning. After that I would fasten his collar to the chain that slid along an overhead wire. This allowed Bill free run of the yard but no more. I took the trouble to leash him for his evening runs only during the twice-monthly times when major Solunar periods arrived between eleven and one. The rest of the month, Bill was allowed to run free. Not once after we took the Solunar periods into account did Bill fail to show up in time to go to bed.

The answer to the mysterious midnight runs is evident. The arrival of a Solunar period is nature's notification that the time for activity and feeding has come. Dogs have enough of their wild traits left so that they respond to Solunar periods by going "on the prowl" for the two-hour interval. Just as your dog will turn around two or three times before lying down on the living-room rug (a heritage from his wild forebears that thus made their beds in the long grass) so he will, as you will learn if you watch him, go on his appointed rounds when a Solunar period is in progress.

Some dogs are quite restless if they are confined to the house during Solunar periods. With young dogs particularly this is noticeable. Leafing through my diary the other day, I found this entry:

> Sunday, April 30th, 1941.—The Solunar period (major) came in the morning about 9.30. Never since we have had him have I seen our puppy, Joe, so filled with ambition. Finally, I had to banish him to the back yard until the activity period had passed and his excess spirits could be worked off. Now, at 12.15, he is sound asleep at my feet and peace is once more restored.

Offsetting this, probably will be the criticism that morning is the normal time for puppies to play anyway. I know that I had it in mind at the time, so I watched Joe carefully for a week or ten days as the Solunar periods arrived later and later in the morning, finally moving over into the afternoon. Watching Joe is not difficult. He and his uncle, Pete—two little lemon-and-white cocker spaniels—practically live in my lap. No matter where I go about the house, these two are on my heels like two little shadows. Only at mealtime (for them) do they desert me in favor of Beth, who feeds them. Once fed, they are under my feet again for the rest of the day.

As I said, I watched Joe carefully for the next week or ten days. Of course, he was lively first thing in the morning as are all healthy youngsters. But as the Solunar periods arrived later in the morning, he often was sound asleep on the floor beside my chair in the office as early as nine or nine-thirty.

And that's another thing about dogs and the Solunar Theory. My two dogs will curl up on the rug near my desk almost any time that I am there. Often they both will go sound asleep so that I actually can walk quietly out of the room without waking them. But I have yet to see either of them asleep during an activity period. They may be lying down, eyes shut, but they are both alert and quick to detect any move that I make, no matter how quiet I am about it.

Two men that I know train bird dogs each year. One of them is a professional and he handles as many as seventy-five or a hundred dogs in a season. The other is an amateur who trains hunting dogs as a hobby. Usually he has a kennel of five or six young dogs to train each fall. Each of these men has learned that not only are more birds turned up during Solunar periods but the dogs themselves seem to be more alert and on the job than they are at other times.

One day, while I was having lunch with a friend at one of our local clubs, a man sat down at our table and joined the conversation.

"I thought you might be interested," he said, "in a new way to put the Solunar Tables to use. We have been conducting a rather informal campaign for the extermination of hunting cats that we find along the roads at night. I carry a "game getter" in the back of my car and when I find a cat hunting in the ditch along the road, it's too bad for that cat."

"At first I noticed that I would find a lot more cats some evenings than I would on other evenings, although there seemed to be little choice so far as the weather was concerned. Then I happened to think of your Solunar Tables and I began checking up. Offhand, I suppose, I find five times as many cats during Solunar periods as I do at other times. As a matter of fact, with the help of your little book, I'm running up quite a score of dead cats this spring."

I can see, before this thing is done, that I will have quite a lot to answer for.

Each year, for the past five or six years, I have attended the annual Sportsmen's Show that is held in February in the Grand Central Palace on Lexington Avenue, New York City. The first and second floors of the building are devoted, largely, to the display of sporting goods but on the third floor are dozens of cages holding wild creatures of all kinds.

How I happened on the idea I do not know, but for the past few years I have been surprising many of my friends with a rather conclusive demonstration of how completely the creatures of the wild respond to the stimulus of Solunar influence.

For the majority of the time, all of the creatures on the third floor spend their time lying on the floors of their cages, either asleep or looking bored to death. The only time to look at the menagerie with any satisfaction at all is during the course of a Solunar period, preferably a major period. Then the animals, birds and reptiles are awake and moving about and it is possible to see them. Most people will not believe me when I tell them the exact time to visit the third floor if they would see the menagerie at its best. Never do they fail to evince surprise when they find that I am right and that the animals and birds are alert and active just when I said they would be. How those unhappy, caged creatures know that a Solunar period has arrived is more than I can say. The Grand Central Palace is built of steel and concrete. All day long, the aisles are jammed with thousands of people, and the noise, confusion and dust must be most unpleasant for the menagerie. But, in spite of all these handicaps, there can be no doubt that every last one of them knows when a Solunar period is in progress, as their behavior at these times is unmistakable.

When observing animals, it must be kept in mind that only the small fry, such as mice, react with anything like the promptness of fish or insects. The larger animals may not show signs of activity for as much as an hour after the fish begin to feed. Solunar influence seems to be a cumulative thing and the greater the creature's capacity for thought, the slower it is to react. If this varying "response lag" is disregarded, it is often difficult to reconcile the results of observations of different kinds of creatures.

CHAPTER NINE

It is not easy at first to detect any effect that Solunar periods exert upon normal human beings. Being creatures capable of thought, we have regulated our lives according to the way we think they should be, entirely independent of any dictates that nature may have set up for us prior to our present "developed" state. Compared with those of an animal or a bird, our senses are dulled so that they are almost useless. By the same token, our perceptions are so blunted that it is amazing that nature's promptings can register sufficiently to exert any influence upon our behavior, one way or the other. Yet register they do, in spite of all we have done or can do to prevent it.

To attempt to check the reaction of an individual against the Solunar periods, from hour to hour throughout the day, is a hopeless process that seldom will bring results of any kind. Too many disturbing factors are present constantly to permit satisfactory observations in this way. Even the psychological effect of knowing that we are being watched is enough to render such observations completely valueless. However, there are ways in which the behavior of an individual can be shown to have been guided by the stimulus of Solunar influence.

Our reflexes or states of being over which we can

exercise little or no control are the chinks in our armor that leave us vulnerable to Solunar influence. For instance, if we are sleepy or if we are wakeful, there is little we can do to alter the situation without the aid of medicine or artificial stimulation. If we are cheerful, so much the better. But if we are not, it is difficult to stimulate an artificial state of good humor. To be sure, a cocktail or two will tend to bring on a more pleasant state of mind, but such treatment is mechanical and not emanating from within.

In the matter of sleeping, Solunar influence plays its part. We all know that sometimes we fall asleep almost as soon as our heads touch the pillow. Other times, we are wakeful and restless and sleep refuses to come. These things seem to happen no matter how active we may have been during a *normal* day. Of course, where some form of activity has been indulged in that is outside the usual routine, then physical exhaustion plays its part so that the ordinary rules of behavior are broken. But where we have been living our normal lives, then, when bedtime arrives, we are sleepy or wakeful according to the decision of old Mother Nature.

The way its works out is this. Suppose your normal time for turning in happens to be between eleven and midnight. If a Solunar period has been in progress for the two hours immediately preceding your retirement, you will find that you will have difficulty getting to sleep. The stimulation of Solunar influence to which you have just been subjected tones up your system to the point where your body does not need or demand rest and sleep. Of course, the behavior of the barometer at the time will play its part in the determination of the *intensity* of this stimulation, just as it shows its effect in the behavior of animals or fish, but, by and large, if other conditions are not too unfavorable, then you will be sleepy or wakeful just as the Solunar schedule happens to decide the matter for you.

The quality of your sleep—whether it is restful sleep or fitful and productive of little genuine rest—seems to depend both upon the Solunar schedule and the behavior of the barometer (with its accompanying arrangement of atmospheric magnetism). To illustrate, assume that your alarm clock is set each morning for seven-thirty. Some mornings you will awake refreshed and glad to greet a new day. Other mornings will find you lethargic, slow to awaken and as tired as you were when you went to bed. As a general rule, you will find that when a Solunar period has been in progress for an hour or so before you awake, you will wake up feeling completely rested and ready for work. When seven-thirty arrives just *before the beginning* of a Solunar period, then it is that you will find it both unpleasant and difficult to get out of bed.

Animals and birds do not disregard the benefits of the Solunar schedule. They take advantage of what nature provides for them and, consequently, are all the better for it. Of course, there is always a certain amount of activity among wild life at dawn and again at dusk.

But the intensity of this activity varies in direct proportion with the favorable or unfavorable status of the Solunar schedule.

If you plan to check up on your personal reactions so far as sleep and the Solunar periods are concerned, don't make the mistake of looking up the Solunar periods beforehand. If you do, you will influence your conclusions in spite of all you can do to prevent it. Keep a record of your reactions and check them against the Solunar schedule afterward. Also, in forming your conclusions, do not neglect to take all other factors into consideration. Artificial stimulation (such as too much coffee), the trend of the barometer, the condition of the weather, your state of mind (worried or calm) — all these things have their effects. If you plan to keep a record of your findings about yourself, be sure to consider all of these factors and make suitable allowances.

Being busy during most of my waking hours, about the only chance I have to do any reading is after I turn in. Some nights I find that I can read indefinitely—right through to breakfast, if I were foolish enough to do so. Other nights I have difficulty reading more than a page or two before growing sleepy. Now, I lead a fairly well-ordered existence. During the winter months my mornings are taken up with my mail and attention to office work. If I must go downtown, I usually do so immediately after lunch. Then I work on manuscripts until about four, sign my mail and take a nap for an hour or so, to be fresh for work in the evening. From two to five hours each evening are spent on manuscripts. That certainly is a quiet existence and a regular one, with just about the same amount of effort being expended on the work of each day. Yet the variation in my bodily need for sleep and rest is astonishing when a careful check on it is kept.

Beth is even more "Solunar conscious" than I am. She responds to a major Solunar period as completely as any trout in my pet Loyalsock Creek. Unless she takes sleeping potions out of all proportion to her size, she just can *not* go to sleep after a Solunar period has been in progress for a couple of hours. Again, if a Solunar period has not been in progress for seven or eight hours prior to the time she turns in (I'm talking about major periods now), then nothing short of an outright calamity will keep her awake. Her life is as well ordered as mine and, try as I will, I can find no other possible explanation of her pronounced tendency to sleep or not to sleep, as the case happens to be.

You know that you feel better, more alive, keen and alert on some days than you do on others. Have you ever noticed that this state of alertness varies as the day progresses? Some mornings you can turn out an inordinate amount of work at your desk. Complex matters that have been bothering you for days seem to clarify themselves so easily that you wonder why the solution had not come to you long ago. Then you go to lunch. Regardless of what you have eaten, you return to your desk with little zest and the afternoon drags interminably.

Conversely, you will have trouble getting under way on other mornings. Your secretary, whom you regard secretly as a pearl without price, seems dull and inattentive. Your employees or associates bother you with stupid questions and nothing goes the way it should. As often as not, this upset condition wears itself out as the day progresses and you finish the afternoon as fresh as a daisy and find that, instead of being content to settle in your easy chair for the evening, you feel more like going places and doings things. When some of these *extreme* days come along, make a note of them, as to time and behavior, and check them later against the Solunar schedule.

Some individuals are extremely sensitive to Solunar influence. In a building where I once had my office, there was an elevator man who was just about as dependable as a copy of the Solunar Tables. Over the months and years that I rode up and down in his car, I found that by speaking to him, observing the manner and tone of his replies and his general behavior, I could come fairly close to telling just how the Solunar schedule stood at the moment without consulting the Solunar Tables. This man, of course, was unusual. As a matter of fact, he is the only individual I have known who shows clean-cut reactions from hour to hour.

We know that insane people are affected by the moon in its monthly phases, at least that is the view of many who are in a position to know what they are talking about. Our word "lunacy" is derived from this phenomenon. Recent experiments seem to indicate that the insane react to the day-to-day cycle of activity periods and rest periods just as do the creatures of the wild. Unfortunately, little work of any real value has

Moon Up - Moon Down

been done on this particular application of the Solunar Theory. It should make an interesting study.

Another phase of the effect of Solunar influence on an individual lies in the variation of the muscular coordination of that individual before, during and after Solunar periods. People, after all, are highly developed mammals and there is no physical reason why they should not respond to Solunar stimulus just as other mammals do, always making allowance for the fact that the senses of the average human are dulled in comparison with those of animals. This intensification of coordination shows up in skeet scores, golf scores, batting averages, and, for that matter, all athletic events. Your own experience will tell you how your golf game or your tennis will vary from day to day. Fortunately the games of your opponents are similarly affected.

With groups of people or with large gatherings such as luncheons, meetings, theatre audiences and so on, Solunar effects are definitely noticeable. In the Real Estate Department of the bank where I was employed, there were at one time one hundred and thirty-seven people. Most of these employees worked together in a large, open office that occupied an entire floor of the building. The collective mental attitude or tempo of that department varied concurrently with the Solunar schedule. Being a member of the department, and also interested in their reactions from a Solunar standpoint, I had ample opportunity to watch them every day of the week for several years. When a Solunar period had been in progress for an hour or two, everybody wore a smile and the hum and bustle indicated that an extraordinary amount of work was being done. Between Solunar periods, the activity would settle down to normal. There would be few smiles and little going about from desk to desk. Sometimes, if the weather were bad and the barometer falling, the group would be almost silent, with only a mild flurry of activity and joviality during the Solunar periods.

Theatrical people know of this group reaction, although I do not recall ever having seen it accounted for in any way. Actors are content to identify the two extremes as "warm house" and "cold house," meaning, of course, responsive and unresponsive audiences. Solunar influence will keep an audience on its mental toes. Laughs are frequent and applause is ready and sustained. Just as it is with a school of fish, response to Solunar influence seems to be contagious among people. Even the actors themselves feel it and the performance comes off with a snap and flash that would be impossible under the adverse conditions of bad weather and unfavorable allocation of Solunar periods. Theatrical producers might do well to take this reaction into account when scheduling their "opening nights." A new play starts on its precarious way with enough handicaps, goodness knows, without the added hazard of exposing it to a "cold house" on the first night of its existence.

I have seen the same cycle work for and against me on the lecture platform. Knowing about it in advance is a help, of course, but it is much easier to talk to a stimulated audience than to a sluggish one. Some years ago I was scheduled to address the Kiwanis Club of Orange, New Jersey. While we were eating our lunch, I noticed that there was a tremendous amount of joviality and calling back and forth between tables. When the time for singing arrived, they fairly made the ceiling bulge with the exuberance of their chorus. I spoke of this to their president, who sat next to me.

"Do they always sing like that?"

"They're pretty good as a rule," he said, "but I don't know when I have heard them sing like they have today."

And there you have it. Prior to that meeting, a major Solunar period had been in progress for about two hours. Weather and barometric conditions had been ideal and the time of the month was the dark of the moon when Solunar influence is at its strongest. No wonder the Kiwanis Club was all good fellowship and sang its collective head off. And I, ungrateful creature that I am, sat there and thought of the trout in the pools and runs of the Brodhead, wishing that I could be wading those cool and friendly waters, fly rod in hand, instead of talking to a lot of men who might or might not be interested in what I had to say about the Solunar Theory.

A few years before this was written, a doctor in Ohio conducted an interesting bit of research. In his work as an obstetrician, he had ample opportunity to collect his data. On the premise that the human animal functions more thoroughly and efficiently during Solunar periods than at other times, he conducted a survey of some two thousand maternity cases to which he had access. Of course, there are far too many intervening factors to have the actual time of birth mean much from a Solunar standpoint. But he reasoned that there should be a relationship there somewhere, so he made inquiry and kept a record of the time of the onset of labor in each of the two thousand cases. His findings showed that, in 56 per cent of these maternity cases, labor had begun during a Solunar period. At first glance, that seems like a small margin, but when you consider that this 56 per cent is included in only six hours out of the twenty-four, it begins to look more convincing. Reduced to the simplest terms, it shows for Solunar periods an efficiency ratio of 9.33 to 2.44—almost four to one.

Salesmen, at least a few of them, are learning that Solunar influence seems to have its effect upon the receptivity of a prospect. Drop into any motion-picture theatre in New York City on a rainy afternoon and you will see that a large percentage of the audience is composed of men—salesmen, for the most part, who have learned that it does not pay to call on a prospect when weather conditions are bad. One insurance salesman of my acquaintance—an ardent angler—carries a copy of the Solunar Tables in his brief case as an integral part of his equipment. He assures me that he gets better results if he plans his important calls in conformance with the Solunar schedule.

Some years ago I received an amusing letter from a man in Philadelphia. He is employed as sales manager of a concern that manufactures envelopes. There was one account—a mail-order house—that had given his company no end of trouble for many years. The buyer was a cross-grained individual who seemed to take great joy in throwing salesmen out of his office. No shipment ever was received without some criticism from him and the account, a large one, carried with it a headache of equal magnitude.

The sales manager, being an angler and familiar with the Solunar Theory, issued orders to his staff that this particular account was not to be called upon, telephoned to or in any way touched without clearance being granted. Then he consulted his Solunar Tables and permitted a salesman to call on this buyer only after a major Solunar period had been in progress for about an hour, and on days that fell during the dark of the moon and the first quarter. After a test period of nearly a year, the record showed that not only had this account given them no trouble during that period; his salesmen had been well received, and the size of the orders had increased.

It is unfortunate that reactions to Solunar influence are not precise, measurable things that take place always with the same intensity and identical characteristics. Uncomplicated by fluctuations in atmospheric pressure, individual temperament, temperature, condition of health and a thousand and one things that go to make the problem complex, our investigations would probably be much more conclusive, from the standpoint of physics, than they are at present. However, we have the advantage of knowing most of the disturbing factors and thus can make allowances for them. In your own observations, providing you are interested enough to make any, always keep these complicating factors in mind. Only in that way can satisfactory results be obtained.

CHAPTER TEN

THE proof of the pudding is in the eating. So far, I have confined this account almost entirely to one man's opinion—my own. Perhaps it might be just as well to see what some other people think about the Solunar Theory.

At the risk of having this chapter sound like a patent-medicine catalogue, these are some of the many hundreds of letters in my "fan-mail" file that might be both amusing and interesting. As I understand the term "fan mail," "fan" is an abbreviation of "fanatic." If that is the case, then "fan mail" most certainly applies to letters about the Solunar Theory. People evidently can't stay lukewarm about it. They denounce it or praise it with all the fervor that can be embraced by the words at their command.

Fan mail seems to vary in length in direct proportion to the writer's temperament and the amount of work he has on hand at the moment. Individually, these letters prove very little: collectively, they add up to such a preponderant mass of confirmatory testimony that their very weight of numbers renders them irrefutable.

Most of them are but a line or two and it is a rare mail indeed that does not contain at least one or two of this variety. Leafing at random through the stack of letters on my desk beside me, I find such things as these—

...have fished every day for ten weeks by your guide, and find that it works perfect.

I might as well leave my rods at home as go vacationing without the tables.

...have more sport and less dissatisfaction than I ever did before I used it.

Have followed it for three years and I have as much sport with less time than I would have had without it.

...a great help to the man whose fishing hours are limited.

Used one last year. Found it right to the minnet. Will bye one every year from now on.

...they bite better on the Solunar time table than at other times.

I use them religiously and they work.

They sure work out fine. I haven't missed once when the air pressure was O.K.

...best general guide to get all there is out of fishing ever conceived.

...I told them in a more or less spirit of fun that I could tell them exactly what time they caught their fish and incidentally did.

Every quail that we killed in three days of hunting was killed during Solunar periods.

I could write all day about the experiences I have had following the tables for both salt and fresh water.

It is needless for me to remind you of their remarkable accuracy.

THEY WORK—100%! [This one was a telegram.]

...taking over 200 small mouth bass on plugs. 90% of them were caught on "Book Time."

If more sportsmen used these tables, they would have fewer disappointments.

I do not know how I could get along without it.

And so on, indefinitely. There are hundreds in my file and many more that have been thrown away, reluctantly, in the interests of conservation of filing space.

Some of the writers are classified in the I-knew-it-all-the-time department. Like this for instance:

> ... they sure are a wonderful book, for that's the way I always fish but I would always have to figure it our for myself.

There is nothing new under the sun.

Not all of these letters are confined to fishing. Here are two that apply to hunting.

> Two of my friends went rabbit hunting Christmas day with a very good hound. They went to a very good place, arriving about 11:30 in the morning. They hunted over a good piece of country without seeing a rabbit and were returning about 2:15 P.M. over the same ground when suddenly the rabbits appeared. They got ten in all before 3:00 o'clock. I made a little bet that the tables would show a major period then. You can imagine my satisfaction on arriving home and checking the time. It was a bulls-eye.

This man's comment is interesting in that it describes so completely the behavior of rabbits during the cold weather. As I have remarked earlier, they stay in their warm warrens most of the time, only coming out to feed with the arrival of a Solunar period.

Here is another one that deals with hunting.

> Since the first of the year (this letter was dated January 15th) my setter has routed two deer on different days. They were feeding high on the hill above the

creek bottom where they yard. As soon as I got my new copy of the Solunar Tables, I checked back on the times. One deer was feeding on the minor period and the other on the major.

The following is a letter that was written by an angler who is well known in salt-water circles for his exploits with tuna and broadbill off Jersey and Block Island. In the spring he does some trout fishing, I imagine to fill in the time until the big fellows are running offshore. A sporting-goods dealer, wishing to have an impartial and reliable opinion on the Solunar Tables, wrote to this man, asking what he thought of them. This is what he answered:

> I am completely sold on Solunar Tables and I have kept track of every fresh and salt-water fish I have caught for three years. Every trout was taken on the table and 95% of the salt-water stuff. The Commercial salt-water fishermen I know arrange their dory launchings so as to be on the grounds on the zero hour and are thoroughly sold.

A good share of my letters are of the business-letter type, terse and to the point. Now and then, however, I receive one that has been written by a man who knows what he wants to say and how to go about saying it.

> Dear Mr. Knight,
> I suppose this is pretty much old stuff to you, but your Solunar Tables work just as well on Texas Bass as they do on Eastern trout. I have used your Solunar tables for the past three years, and a check shows me that over 90% of my fish were caught during Solunar Periods.

Moon Up - Moon Down

One day last Summer when the local fishing seemed to have gone definitely to the bow-wows, and no fish were being caught by anybody, I discovered that the Solunar Tables showed that the fish would bite between 12:30 noon and 2:30 that afternoon, and as I could get off at that time, I grabbed my rod and made for the local lake, only a short drive away.

When I arrived at the lake a bunch of the boys were lying in the shade panting—it was Mid-Summer and hot enough to bake your brains out—and when they saw me assembling my rod and getting ready to go fishing, they gasped in amazement. They knew me well enough to know that I was no "book fisherman," but a hard-headed guy who could out and get his fish with any of them, and they didn't know what to make of it. They had been out at daybreak, throwing everything but a quarter's worth of pork chops at the bass, and had no luck whatever, and were waiting to see if the durn things would bite at sundown. And when they saw I proposed to go out in the middle of a blazing, cloudless day, when the fish weren't biting anyway, well, they quite frankly opined that the heat had finally gotten me, and I had blown my topper.

I rowed out to a weed bed a short distance away and started casting. It was so hot that I was sousing my head with water, and as I was wearing canvas sneakers, I had to keep sticking my feet over the side to cool them off. Yet in less than an hour I was back at the dock with three beautiful bass, and you should have seen the expressions on the faces of those wise guys. And to add the complete and finishing touches to their ignominy, two old ladies who had been anchored to a stump, dunking minnows for crappie not far from where I had been casting, both landed a bass weighing better than two pounds while I was casting.

Naturally they asked me how come, and I showed them my Solunar Tables, and explained what you said about the fish sometimes biting during the middle of the day during the dark of the Moon, and I made some Solunar converts then and there. After all, you can't quarrel with results.

The receipt of a letter like that makes up for quite a few hard knocks from other sources.

Not all fan mail is sent to me, particularly if it happens to be of a critical nature. A good share of that sort goes to the newspaper columnists or to the editors of the outdoor magazines. One fellow from Sterling, Kansas, had a lot of fun writing to the editor of *Outdoor Life*, kidding him, and me, about one of my articles on the Solunar Theory. Neither the editor nor I did anything about that letter. We didn't have to. A champion of the Solunar Theory read the critic's letter when it was published in *Outdoor Life* and he took up the cudgels in my defense. They had quite a time of it, calling names in the pages of each edition of the magazine for some time afterward.

There is still another class of fan mail, one that is designed to make my life miserable. That they do not succeed is perhaps the most favorable commentary of all on the reliability of the Solunar Theory. Beth and I refer to them as "guess-when" letters.

In their milder form, the "guess-when" letters are like this one.

On July 28, 1937, at 7 A.M. (Daylight Saving Time), I caught a 28 pound striped bass from the sea. [He had

Moon Up - Moon Down

given me his fishing location previously in the letter.] Could you inform me as to the time you recorded the major Solunar period for that day?

I replied that the major period for that day was from 5.55 A.M. to 7.55 A.M., daylight time, showing that the bass was caught on schedule. The gentleman was kind enough to order a copy of the Solunar Tables.

The more formidable "guess-when" letters are not as liberal with information as the one about the striped bass. The following one is more true to type, the idea being to put me "on the spot" good and solid before telling me how wrong I am about fish and their habits. I am quoting this series *in toto*, all but the name and address.

Dear Sir:—
Not wanting to buy a pig in a poke I would like to test your Solunar Tables on actual fishing trips.
On July 1st, 1939, I fished nearly all day and got the most fish, in fact all the fish in 1½ hours.
On July 4th all were caught in about 1 hour. Can you tell me the time this happened. If your book tallies with these days I will buy one.

I happened to be away on an extended vacation when this letter arrived, but my secretary, who had seen quite a few of these letters, took it upon herself to answer it. This is the reply that we received after he had read her letter.

Dear Sir:
On the two days I ask about, the first and fourth of July. The actual time the fish, small mouth bass,

started to hit was 1:30 P.M. The Solunar Tables said 1:40 P.M., ten minutes difference.

On July [4th] they hit at 3:00 P.M. the table said 3:20 P.M. Very close, close enough that every fisherman should invest 50c in the book.

Written across the top of this last is a note from my secretary. "Boy! Am I relieved. I sent the right times. Missy."

Of the many "guess-when" letters that I have received, I think that I have been able to state the times of the best fishing at least in 95 per cent of the cases presented. Now and then I'll miss, but not often and usually by a reasonably narrow margin. More frequently I find that the Solunar Tables are exactly right.

The reason for this high percentage of accuracy is not obscure. Usually I am called upon to indicate the time of day when large numbers of fish were caught—record catches. For a man to make a record catch of fish, he must have record conditions existing at the time—favorable weather, temperatures, water conditions and so on. Moreover, included in these other advantageous conditions must be that vital one, *i.e.*, that the fish are disposed to feed. Other conditions not being unfavorable, the fish will feed during Solunar periods and, as a rule, I can't miss.

Only once have I had a "guess-when" letter sent to an editor. The writer was not acquainted with the Solunar Tables, but he had read an article about the Solunar Theory, so he wrote to the editor of *Outdoor Life*, stating his case and requesting that it be passed along to me. His letter, in part, was as follows:

Moon Up - Moon Down   115

Here is one I wonder if he could answer. Was hunting deer last fall in Northern Michigan. Hunted continuously without success from Nov. 15th until Thanksgiving. On Thanksgiving I killed a 200 pound buck. There was no other hunter in the neighborhood, and the buck was just sauntering around. What time of day did I kill him?

That is a rather tough assignment. It is not difficult to predict what a large group of animals or fish will be doing at a certain time of a certain day. Group reaction is quite clean-cut and nearly always runs true to form. But the behavior of one animal alone, and that animal a deer that has lived through two weeks of the hunting season, is more than likely to be influenced by many extraordinary factors. However, the writer of the letter stated that he was the only hunter in the neighborhood. Also he said that the buck was "just sauntering around." Evidently the animal had not been disturbed or frightened and was going about his ordinary daily business. At all events, I had to assume that he was. I wrote to the man, after consulting my Solunar Tables, and said that he should have killed his buck at about eight o'clock in the morning, Standard time. This is the reply, again in part:

You sure did it. And I want to congratulate you. The time was 9:00 A.M., daylight saving time [which, of course, is 8:00 A.M., Standard time]. I could hardly believe my eyes when I opened your letter.

Fan mail has taught me a number of important things and it has found many friends for me in various parts of the globe. Before this beastly war broke out, I had active correspondents in England, Scotland, France, Chile, Peru, Panama, Hawaii, Norway, Finland, Iceland, China, the Philippines, North Africa, South Africa, New Zealand and Australia. From fan mail I have become acquainted with the huchen and the grayling of the mountain torrents of Austria and Bavaria or what used to be Austria and Bavaria before Schickelgrüber and his Third Reich took over. I have learned of the habits and phenomenal growth of the brown trout and the rainbow of Australia, New Zealand, Chile and Peru. In my files are snapshots of monster catfish, Goliath and Nile perch from the waters of the upper Nile in North Africa. I have taken imaginary fishing trips in quest of crayfish and stone crabs on the reefs off British Honduras; for exotic salt-water denizens with my Chinese friend from Penang, Straits Settlements; for hognosed mullet in the picturesque mountain streams of the island of Jamaica. Some day, when the world is once more a fit place in which to live, I may visit these places. Until then these fish will live in the bright waters of my imagination where their pictures have been painted by the writers of my ever-growing file of fan mail.

It is extremely gratifying now and then to find a man who can appreciate the *full* use of the Solunar Tables. This letter came one day, all unannounced, and I have treasured it ever since. A man must love and understand the outdoors to be able to write a letter like this one.

I have so much to say to you about my experiences

Moon Up - Moon Down

with the Solunar Tables that the biggest problem will be boiling it down.

I've slipped into a patch of woods and sat down when seemingly there wasn't a living thing in the woods. This breathless silence would continue until the Solunar period would come in. Then rather gradually the whole woods would come to life. Birds would begin to sing and move around, squirrels would go on the move, evidentally in search of food.

North of us in Kiscinsko County lies Wawasee Lake, the largest in the state. Around this large lake at various points, canals or "slips" have been constructed, serving as passageways for boats from cottages located back a ways from the lake. These canals are shallow and the bass move into them in the Spring. When the water rises to a certain temperature, they will strike a top-water bait after dark.

One night five of us went up to one of these canals on Wawasee, arriving there about seven-thirty P.M. We fished hard from then until about eleven P.M. before any of us got a strike. At eleven P.M. the major Solunar period came in and the bass began to strike furiously until about one A.M. Had I not known about Solunar periods we would undoubtedly have quit and come home before the period came in.

On April 16th this year, I landed 13 bass on a Dardevle Imp during Solunar time. Three of these fish went home with me and the rest went back in the water so they'd be there next time, maybe. On this particular day there were a lot of ducks on the lake and I remarked to my partner that when the Solunar period came in, the air seemed full of flying ducks. Before this time they had all been sitting on the water. I have noticed from time to time that during a Solunar period ducks are restless and on the move.

Recently I purchased one of the new barometers and I believe with the aid of this instrument and the Solunar Tables I will have most of the answers.

There is no doubt that this man drains to its dregs his cup of enjoyment in the outdoors. Surely, he gets his money's worth out of his Solunar Tables. Songbirds, animals, ducks and fish, all in one letter! Evidently to him has been given the priceless gift of the power to observe. All too few of us have it. Even though I have schooled myself in observation for fifteen years or better, I often miss important things. My young son taught me that the character of the wind—the way in which it blows, not the direction—changes with alterations in barometric pressure. "It was a nice day, Dad," he said, "with the wind *high in the trees.*" The difference in winds had not been evident to me before, even though I had known for years that leaves turning over in the wind are sure indications of lowering atmospheric pressure with probable rain to follow. Then the wind is low, next to the ground, but I had never noticed. Without doubt, we all look at things, but very few of us *see* them.

And, while we are at it, here is another admission. I, who thought I had covered about all of the physical manifestations of Solunar influence, have been taught one more aspect of it by a man who must have keener powers of observation than I ever can hope to possess. This is his letter:

> I believe this is the fourth or fifth year that I am getting this little book, and I am learning more about

it every year. I wish I had time to tell you of all of the interesting experiences that I have had with that little book. I am a night man in a garage, and there are hours during the night when I have nothing to do except watch the activity of the public, the dogs, the birds and even the wind. No matter how calm the waters may be, when the time comes for an active period, I can always win myself a lunch from anyone that wants to bet with me on a breeze for a short time by the clock.

This is the first intimation that I have had that the Solunar periods and atmospheric movements are in any way connected.

Long ago, I stopped being surprised at the things that turn up in my fan mail. Surprise has given way to curiosity, wondering what the next mail will bring.

CHAPTER ELEVEN

When the Solunar Theory was first made public, we were somewhat surprised at the way in which it was received. Perhaps it would be more accurate to say that the real surprise lay in the way in which it was *not* received in certain quarters. Here and there, self-appointed critics turned up who seemed to take a great deal of pleasure in ridiculing the whole idea. Most of these skeptics in the vicinity of New York City developed from the ranks of those I had known and with whom I had fished for years—my friends. A prophet is not without honor, save in his own country. These men were glad to have flies tied by me in preference to those available at the tackle shops. Many of them sought my advice in matters of equipment and came to me with their casting troubles. But they smiled indulgently at the Solunar Theory and refused to have any part of it, much less give it a fair trial. I couldn't understand it then and I can't now.

For many years I was a member of one of the oldest sportsmen's clubs in New York City. For a while I sat on its Board of Directors and for five years was chairman of its House Committee, worrying myself over servants, furnishings, food and so on. There were only a few of its several hundred members whom I did not know by their first names. Naturally, when I had spent enough time on the Solunar Theory to know that it was both sound and practical, I assumed that I could depend upon my fellow club members to lend a hand in bringing the Solunar schedule up to a state of perfection in a hurry. It was this very group that formed the most solid wall of resistance during the first year or so that I strove to break down the barriers of unbelief in what I knew to be the truth.

One of my most outright critics was a man with whom I had fished for many years. Being an angler of national reputation in his own right, it may have been that he disliked having me advance a theory that would leave its lasting mark on angling history, once it became established. I may be doing him a grave injustice in this belief, but, try as I will, I can find no other reason. Eventually, he set out to disprove it, once and for all time. He arrived at his final decision after two rather amusing reversals of attitude.

Before making the Solunar Theory public property, I decided to spend one more season checking it against the behavior of the trout and bass in the streams that I fished—when I found the opportunity to go fishing. Feeling that two heads always are better than one, I told this man what was in my mind and asked him to help me. He listened until I had finished.

"The whole idea is crazy," he said. "There is no possible phenomenon known to science that could cause a feeding-and-rest cycle like that. Trout feed when there's a hatch drifting. No hatch—no feeding. Forget it and go to work on something practical."

Evidently I would get no help from that source, so I said no more about it and made what observations I could.

The following January the Solunar Theory was introduced and the first Solunar Tables were printed in April. I gave one of them to my friend. Early in May we met at an appointed spot to spend two days together, trout fishing. He had arrived the day before and was at work with his fly rod when I drove up the next morning. He greeted me with a broad smile.

"Your book's no good," he said. "The trout have been five minutes behind schedule for the past two days."

"Have you been checking up on the Solunar periods?" I asked. "Joking aside, how close do they come to being right?"

"They're pretty good," he said. "I've checked them fairly regularly since the first of the season and darned if I don't think you've got something."

Two weeks later another friend of mine met him while trout fishing. He asked him what he thought of the Solunar Tables.

"They're all right," was the reply. "We've just about got this thing licked."

That "we" business went on for about another month, but the Solunar Tables still were mentioned as "Jack Knight's Solunar Tables." The strain was too great. One day, after the trout season was well advanced, he came storming into the club and started to take me to task almost before he was inside the door.

There were about twenty men present but that didn't discourage him any.

"Jack," he said, "that book of yours is no damn good. I've checked it nearly every day of the season and it doesn't mean a thing."

Then he proceeded to make a speech to the entire assembly. He recounted his experiences, told them how wrong I was and wound up by showing how the law of averages would make me guess right 25 per cent of the time anyway, regardless of any calculations I might make. I suppose he expected me to rise in the defense of my pet theory. Instead, I smiled, expressed surprise and went on eating my lunch. And there the matter died, at least for the time being.

As the years passed and the Solunar Theory became more firmly established, his tirades grew less scathing. To this day I am not sure whether or not he knows that the Solunar schedule is all that I claim it to be.

As might be expected, the Solunar Theory was not taken seriously by the various angling clubs of the Catskills, the Poconos and the Adirondacks. To be sure, it was the basis of many a fireside argument during the trout seasons of 1935 and 1936. However, most of those anglers held it to be outright nonsense and would have nothing to do with it. But there were some men in each of these clubs who were open-minded enough to give it a trial. Gradually, the Solunar Theory became less and less funny. Now many of these clubs keep a copy of the Solunar Tables tacked to the bulletin board throughout the season. To be sure, there are still some of their members who will not take the trouble to find out the times of the Solunar periods from day to day, but these are fewer in number as the years pass. It takes time to convince everybody.

The columnists and outdoor writers of the country have, by and large, been eminently fair in their reception of the Solunar Theory. Only in a few cases has it been ridiculed in print by any of these professional writers. They have made it known to their readers, largely as a matter of news, and have given it an unbiased presentation.

Many of their readers, however, have not behaved as well. Some of their letters have been rather strident, condemning it for utter damn nonsense and taking the columnist to task for printing an account of it. A goodly share of these letters are sent to me for reply and I try to handle them as tactfully as possible. Often it is a bit difficult to write an even-tempered answer to a man who has just called you an idiot and a nature-faker. I used to get all upset over some of them. Fortunately they do not arrive very frequently these days.

Now and then I find a man who declines to use the Solunar Tables because he goes fishing when he can find the time and fishes all day every time he goes out. That strikes me as rather faulty reasoning. If an angler —or a hunter—can know in advance what time to expect the day's best fishing or when the birds will be in the feeding cover, surely it is possible for him to plan his days in the open more intelligently than if he just trusts to luck. A glance at the Solunar Tables will tell him whether the fish will be in the shallows or in deep water. Most men think that they fish all day when they go fishing, but the truth of the matter is that they don't. They are bound to spend some time going from place to place. They take time out for lunch, have a spare tire repaired, go to the nearest store for cigarettes—there are many things that will take a fisherman away from his fishing, at least for a little while. How much more sensible it is to get these odd jobs done when you *know* that you are not apt to miss the high spot of the day by doing them at just the wrong time.

Now and then I find it possible to have a little fun with one of my critics by showing him how he has been using the Solunar Theory for years without knowing it. There are two fellows who live in the metropolitan district who are ardent "night-fishermen." One day I happened to meet both of them at the club and they joined in a little mild kidding about the "Solunatic Theory." When they had about run down, I asked the older of the two:

"What time is best for fishing at night? How do you know when to start out?"

"Are you joking?" he asked.

"Not at all," I said. "I just like to compare notes, that's all."

"Well," he said, after a little thought, "I don't know what the experience of you two fellows has been, but when I go night-fishing, I want the night to be dark—dark as possible, with no moon in the sky. I usually get to the stream about eleven o'clock and fish until three or four in the morning. That's when I seem to have the best luck."

The other man said that his experience had been about the same. I waited until they had agreed upon the best time for night-fishing; then I dropped my little surprise into their laps.

"You fellows seem to agree that dark nights, with no moon in the sky, between the hours of eleven and four, furnish the best conditions. Let's see just how that works out. Dark nights—no moon in the sky—the only time you get those nights is during the dark of the moon. At that time of the month the major Solunar periods arrive at some time between the hours of eleven and four." (I showed them the Solunar Tables to prove my point.) "What you two have been doing all these years has been to plan your fishing so that you made full use of the midnight Solunar periods. In other words, you have been stanch advocates of the 'Solunatic Theory' all these years without realizing it. Isn't it about time that you look into the matter a little more thoroughly?"

In the winter of 1940, I ran across a man whom I had known for years. We were at the annual Sportsmen's Show and I was watching the contests in the tank when somebody slapped me on the shoulder. I was glad to see him after losing track of him for so many years, so we found a quiet corner and sat down to talk over old times. During the war, we had been stationed at Pensacola, Florida, where we had shot quail and dove, fished for bass and cruised about the bays and inlets, casting plugs for sea trout and channel bass. When the war was over, I met him again in New York, where, at one time, we worked for the same company. We spent many week-ends together, fishing for trout in the Spring and shooting ducks on Long Island Sound in the Fall. Then the depression came and he disappeared. It developed that he owned and operated a game farm up in Connecticut where he provided railbird and duck shooting together with upland game shooting. He said that he had been reading my things in the outdoor magazines, had intended to write but somehow never got around to it.

"By the way," he said, "what's all this Solunar Tables business of yours? Is there anything to it?"

I explained it to him briefly and how it worked out, both for fishing and hunting.

"Do you really think that it works out with ducks?" he asked.

"Certainly," I answered. "I have been watching ducks respond to Solunar periods for several years down in Chesapeake Bay."

"Up our way," said my friend, "the ducks fly on a certain stage of tide. I always try to have my gunners in the blinds so that they can take advantage of those tidal flights. That's when they get the real shooting."

He told me what stage of tide he had in mind, so, just for curiosity, we went to one of the booths that sponsored salt-water fishing and secured a copy of the tide tables for Long Island Sound. Sure enough, the particular stage of tide during which the ducks were active in his locality coincided with the major Solunar periods.

The refusal by many skeptical anglers to have any faith in the Solunar Theory has always been a mystery to me. Every angler wants to know when the fish are going to feed. All of them are anxious to catch big fish. If only they would listen to reason, they could have so much more fun than they do.

Big fish are hard to hook and, once hooked, they are hard to land, because they are stronger than the smaller fish and are capable of breaking tackle or tearing free. There is a clean-cut reason why big fish feed less often and are difficult to interest in what you have to offer them. The matter explains itself about in this way.

When a fish is small, nature prompts him to eat plenty of food so that he can grow, put on weight and be of proper size when he reaches maturity. Like all young things, he has a good appetite and is fairly active most of the time. A young trout, to gain a pound in weight, must consume about ten pounds of the food that is available in a trout stream—usually insects. It takes a lot of insects to make ten pounds of food, and a youngster must hustle to find enough to satisfy his insatiable appetite. Thus, with reasonably satisfactory weather and conditions, we can catch small trout almost any time.

Once a trout has arrived at maturity—four to five years of age—and has attained his weight, his habits change. Instead of insects being the major portion of his diet, he turns cannibalistic and preys on smaller fish, crustaceans, frogs and so on. Contrary to popular opinion, however, it is seldom that an adult trout will make the effort to capture and eat one of his own species. It is much easier for him to catch a riffle chub or minnow. It requires about one pound of food per year to support and keep healthy a pound of trout. Thus, an adult trout can cut down his activity and his feeding to about 10 per cent of what it was when he was growing up. In other words, it is ten times as difficult to hook a large trout as it is to hook a small one. The use of flies builds up the odds against you even higher, because an adult trout is not usually interested in flies.

The one time of the day when a big trout is apt to feed is during a Solunar period. Then is the time that Nature tells him there will be hellgrammites crawling on the rocks in the riffles, crayfish will come out of hiding and minnows will be moving about in the shallows. Then he can obtain a meal with a minimum of effort and, naturally, he will feed at these times if he is going to feed at all that day. Why, then, not fish for him when he is most apt to be in a receptive mood? All you have to do is look up the time in your tables before you start out in the morning.

Several men have gone to considerable trouble to disprove the Solunar Theory in articles that have been published in magazines from time to time. There was one fellow who published his findings in some research he did while fishing the Au Sable of Michigan. He kept a record, day by day, for an entire month, and I must say that the score looked unfavorable for me at first glance. Then I read the article more carefully and the answer was clear.

He had conducted his campaign during the month of July. The trout that he caught were small trout, little better than fingerlings, and he had done no night-fishing, at least he did not speak of it in his report. Those three items are all important.

As luck would have it, I have fished the very waters whereon this experiment was made. Moreover, I have fished them in the month of July. I have talked to many of the Michigan anglers who fish the Au Sable and I have gossiped with the local fishermen and am acquainted with their methods.

The Au Sable is a shallow, flat-bottomed stream at this point. It flows through short riffles and long quiet pools, exposed without cover to the hot July sun. During the day and well into the evening, water temperatures of 72° to 76° are not uncommon. I have fished for trout for over forty years, but I have never seen Eastern adult trout active and feeding in that temperature range.

In addition, the state has conducted a stream-improvement project there and the waters are bountifully supplied with stocked trout, ranging in size from four to seven inches. These little fellows are busy all the time and activity on their part does not mean a whole lot. I found them as active as could be when my stream thermometer registered 73° Fahrenheit.

Through July the local anglers fish only at night. Then the water cools off so that the trout can move and feed in comfort. We went to the Au Sable intending to spend a week or two. When we found out what the fishing conditions were, we left the day after our arrival. My critic might have profited by doing likewise.

Perhaps the most active group of critics of the Solunar Theory is composed of the members of one of the oldest angling clubs in Great Britain. Why they should go to such lengths to discredit fifteen years of work on the part of a fellow angler, I am not prepared to say. The fact remains that they have made repeated attacks on the Solunar Theory, *all* of them not only unwarranted but unsound.

To give you some idea, their most comprehensive condemnation was the review of the day-to-day record of a salmon fisherman who logged in a notebook the exact time that he hooked each fish that he caught. This log was meticulously kept for two complete fishing seasons.

The man who wrote the article was kind enough to send me the original log. I prepared a chart, showing the twenty-four-hour span, extending over the number of days covered by the two fishing seasons. Across this chart, I plotted colored bands, to show the progress of the Solunar periods from day to day, and then I set in the time that each separate fish was hooked. According to my findings, 54 per cent of those salmon were hooked during Solunar periods. Then I sent the log and the chart to London.

Beth tells me that one of my most grievous faults (among the many that she can point out from time to time) is that I always take too much for granted. Certainly, she was right about that in this case. I assumed that the record would speak for itself and that my correspondent, when writing his article, would present all of the facts.

Not being content to accept my figures, he replotted the chart and showed that approximately 48 per cent of the salmon were hooked during Solunar periods. Then he went on to say that, as he had suspected all along, the Solunar Theory was only one more of the fanciful ideas about angling that would not bear too close inspection. The editor of the club bulletin, in which this article was published, wrote a rather scathing editorial wherein he said that the writer of the article had "scotched this snake" so that it could be buried and forgotten as all such carrion should be.

Well—I'm content to accept my critic's figures of 48 per cent. Let's take a look at the way in which his calculations actually work out.

In the first place, six hours of the twenty-four (approximately) are included in the Solunar periods. Figuring that 48 per cent of the salmon were hooked during these six hours as against 52 per cent in the remaining 18 hours, this reduces to an efficiency ratio of 8 to 2.88 in favor of Solunar periods as compared with other times.

More simply, the likelihood of hooking a salmon in that stream, at least during those two seasons, was 2¾ times as probable during Solunar periods as it was at other times. Those odds, it seems to me, would make

Moon Up - Moon Down

the Solunar Tables a worth-while little book to have in your kit when you go fishing.

Now, let us take the matter a step farther. It must be remembered that this is the record of *one* rod. Once a salmon is hooked it takes anywhere from twenty minutes to an hour to bring him to net or gaff, depending on his size and fighting ability. Suppose we assume that this angler was both powerful and adroit and that he landed his fish in an average time of twenty minutes. That reduces itself to an efficiency ratio of 10.9 to 3.1 in favor of the Solunar periods, a little better than three and a half to one. My suggestion is that they "unscotch" that "snake" and adopt it as a club mascot.

I had a letter from a member of this club that expresses their attitude better than anything I could say. The letter speaks for itself. He said, in part:

> It seems inconceivable to me that such a cycle of feeding periods should exist. If it *did* exist, I feel sure that one of our members would have discovered it long since.

The crowning achievement of that group, however, was the publication, in their bulletin in 1937, of the account of a "discovery" on the part of one of their members. This man is, or was then, a member of a well-known salmon-fishing club. On the table in the club lounge stood a bowl of water in which swam some goldfish. He "discovered" that when these little fish were active and swimming about in their glass bowl, the salmon in the river also would be active and that was the time when fishing was at its best. This identical reaction or similarity of behavior was discussed in the April, 1935, issue of the *Sportsman*—the issue in which the second installment of the article introducing the Solunar Theory was published—and I don't remember how many times it has been mentioned since then, both in books and magazine articles. I've stopped worrying about my fellow anglers in London. It produces too little return for the effort involved.

A friend of mine in Canada—a feature writer for one of the newspapers—is an amateur naturalist in his off time. He is a good newspaperman and just as good a naturalist. He knows the trees and the flowers by their generic names and the song of a bird brings to him the same degree of identification that a friend's name, address and telephone number brings to me. He fishes and hunts enthusiastically, not so much for the fish that he may catch or the game he may kill—although he enjoys that too—but for the joy of being in the out-of-doors and of partaking of the bounties Nature has to offer us. He maintains—and I agree with him—that a man who takes with him a fishing rod or a gun will learn more of nature and its creatures in one day than a man who merely goes for a walk in the woods will learn in a year.

One sparkling spring morning, he and two of his friends went trout fishing. Beside the stream, my friend found, nestled among the rocks on a hillside, a bed of Canadian anemones. He stopped to look at them and, as he did so, an idea came to him. While his fly rod rested safely among the protecting branches of a sapling, he knelt beside that glorious little blanket of green and white and counted the blooms. He counted them carefully and his reckoning showed 217 blooms open and 76 blooms partly open. That was at seven-thirty in the morning.

The major Solunar period that day came at eleven-thirty. Just before eleven-thirty he counted the blooms again. There were 234 fully open and 81 partly open —an increase of 17 mature blooms and 5 immature ones. Two hours later, at the close of the Solunar period, he counted them a third time. This time there were 304 fully open and 130 partly open—an increase of 70 and 49 respectively. At six that evening he counted them a fourth time and found that the warm spring afternoon had opened 22 more blooms fully while 13 more were partly open.

Elated over his findings, he related his experience to a professional naturalist. The naturalist laughed scornfully, and said,

"Don't you realize that at high noon, most buds would open to bloom?"

So he sought out promptly a second practical naturalist in his office in a great university. To him he related his experience, only this time he lied and said that the large increase in blooms had happened at eight o'clock in the morning. This man laughed too and patted him on the shoulder.

"Don't you realize," he said, "that at eight in the morning, by which time the day is full, most plants do their most active blooming?"

Still to a third naturalist he told the story, this time fixing the active blooming at seven o'clock in the evening. This man smiled tolerantly and shook his head.

"Don't you realize that at evening, when the day's heat is done, most plants bloom most actively?"

One thing that every outdoor person does know is that there are noons as still and motionless as there are noons full of life: that these hours of activity in nature have no set time from day to day, as we figure time by the rising and setting of the sun. But on days much alike in all else, these hours of activity, of intensity, joy and awareness, come without evident cause and cease as abruptly and inexplicably as they have come. We may or may not have found the cause of these things. That remains to be seen. Now, at least, we can tell you in advance when to expect them.

CHAPTER TWELVE

SINCE the beginning of man, the moon has been credited with being the cause of countless phenomena. So many happenings in nature are timed in its rhythm that it is not surprising that the moon should be held responsible for their very existence. A discussion of all of the beliefs regarding the moon not only would be impracticable here but impossible as well. There are far too many of them for that. Besides, there are excellent books that are devoted entirely to that subject. But there are some beliefs about the moon that seem to fit into this discussion quite properly.

So far as we know, the moon, *of itself*, is responsible for none of the many phenomena with which it has been credited. Even the ocean tides are not *directly* attributable to the moon, and the sun. The *direct* cause of the tides is the gravitational attraction exerted by these heavenly bodies, they, in reality, functioning only as catalyzing agents in the more liberal sense. Viewed in this light, it is entirely possible that the moon may have more to do with some of the things that go on about us from day to day than might be expected at first glance.

Since the time of the ancient Romans, the moon has been held responsible for the growth of living things. A waxing moon (from the dark of the moon to the full moon) has always been considered to be beneficial to growth. A waning moon (from full moon until dark of the moon) was supposed to retard growth. Things born or planted during a waxing moon were thought to be healthy, while the reverse was true of those planted or born during a waning moon. Palladius, a Roman authority on farming, advised planting during a waxing moon and reaping during a waning moon. Pliny, in his writings, mentions the moon's effects, calling attention to the fact that the Emperor Tiberius would have his hair cut only during a waxing moon. The old fellow's hair was getting a little thin and he wanted to stimulate growth if possible. Sheep were shorn during a waxing moon so that their fleece would grow again rapidly. Children and animals that were born during the waxing moon were considered superior and possessed of excellent prospects for healthy growth and robust maturity. Long ago there was a law in France that prohibited the felling of trees except during a waning moon, the theory being that timber cut during a waxing moon would soon rot and not give good service. Just about this single phase of the matter alone—that of growth—there were hundreds of similar rules and superstitions.

A surprisingly large number of these rules of the moon regarding growth have persisted down through the ages. Much like the old home remedies, they exist today and are given as much credence as they were in the days of the Roman emperors. As late as 1928, railroad ties in Cuba had to be cut during a waning moon to qualify for use. No doubt the same rule holds good today. Only last month I had a talk with a foreman of one of the lumber crews that used to drive logs down the Susquehanna River while there was still timber on our mountains forty or fifty years ago. He gave me an old red-oak "wedge" (the sharpened peg that was driven into a log so that it could be tied to a raft). This wedge is forty years old at least and even now is as hard as iron.

"There's a trick about making wedges so they'll last," he said. "Red oak is best but it must be cut two days before the dark of the moon. Otherwise it will rot inside of a year."

This rule of the Pennsylvania lumberman agrees with the old French law and the stipulation for Cuban railroad ties.

Many farmers to this day follow the rules of planting and reaping laid down by Palladius when the world was much younger. Today the rule is not confined merely to crops and farming but has been extended and is used in business as well. I know, personally, two Wall Street bankers who would not dream of entering a new business venture during a waning moon. An associate of mine assured me that he knows many more—men who hold highly paid executive positions in banking houses in "the Street"—who feel the same way about it. Important bond issues, formations of new corporations, any transaction requiring keen judgment or extensive financing is always carried over and completed during the waxing moon.

The first scientific attempt of any consequence (at least, so far as I can discover) to learn more of the actual effects of the moon on living things was made by a Swedish scientist named Svante Arrhenius about fifty years ago. After some years of experimentation, Arrhenius put his finger right on the pulse of the whole thing. He found that atmospheric electricity varies in quantity in a rhythmical manner, timed with the moon, and that the maximum amount occurs at the dark of the moon or, more aptly, at the start of the waxing moon.

The findings of Arrhenius have been contested in view of more recent discoveries of the effects of the sun upon atmospheric and terrestrial magnetism. The rhythmical variation that Arrhenius attributed to the 27⅓-day period of the moon's journey around the earth is now accounted for, at least in some quarters, by the 27-day rotation period of the sun. Be that as it may, there appears to be no doubt that there is a rhythmical variation in magnetism.

In 1938, a report was published in London that listed the results of a number of experiments with plant growth. The experimenter, Mr. L. Kolisko, shows rather conclusively that crops planted two days before the full moon (at the close of the waxing period) grow faster and are productive of better harvests than crops planted two days later or, for that matter, in any other phase of the moon. A Kenya farmer reports an increase of 30 to 40 per cent in his crops by using this method. Now, despite the war, the British Government and the Royal Horticultural Society are conducting extensive experiments along this line.

These things, of course, are all "second-handed" observations, in a manner of speaking. I have not seen them in operation and, therefore, must be content to accept the findings of others. Sometimes that is satisfactory; just as frequently it is not.

There are instances of the effects of lunar cycles upon living things of which I feel qualified to speak with "first-handed" authority. Having watched them in operation for a number of years, I am familiar with their aspects and their peculiarities.

General opinion among anglers seems to be reasonably unanimous (as much so as is possible among the followers of a sport that is noted for its lack of unanimity) that better fishing will be found during the dark of the moon and the first quarter than at other times of the month. Then the moon and the sun are both on the same side of the earth and, being more or less in line, they exert their influence in conjunction rather than in opposition. Thus, during this phase of the moon, Solunar influence seems to be at its maximum. Not knowing what "Solunar influence" is or of what it is composed, there is no way to measure it. The only gauge of its intensity lies in the *results* of this intensity, as evidenced by the behavior of fish and (observed more recently) animals, birds, reptiles, plants, etc. There is no doubt that activity increases during the dark of the moon and the first quarter. Response to Solunar periods is more emphatic and the activity lasts longer than it does during Solunar periods at other times.

From time to time, reports of record catches are sent

to me, either as a matter of interest or as a challenge to the Solunar Theory. Other reports of record catches are found in the outdoor magazines and, when possible, the times of their taking are noted carefully. I suppose that I have checked up on hundreds of them. These reports do not all run true to form and there are exceptions now and then that neither prove the rule or make any sense at all in the light of what we have learned of the great majority of similar cases. Be that as it may, *almost all* of the record catches of fish have three common characteristics. They are taken during the dark of the moon. They are taken during the middle of the day, between the hours of 11 A.M. and 4 P.M. Last but not least, they are taken during major Solunar periods.

Nothing in nature happens without a reason — at least, it does not continue to happen with any degree of regularity. These phenomenal catches of fish of all kinds would not *continue* to be taken at the same times of day and month, year after year, unless there were a sound, basic reason for it. And here is another surprising fact about these record catches. During the months of June, July and August, when most of the record catches are made, a large majority of the fishermen knock off about noon and are content to sit in the shade, eat lunch, take a nap or whatnot until the day's heat is past. Consequently, only a small percentage of the available anglers are actually fishing at the time these record catches are made. By the law of averages, more record catches should be made in the early morning or in the evening, when all of the available rods are fishing. This, however, is not the case. Astonishingly few record catches are made in the early morning or after sundown, even though these very times are generally considered to be the high spots of each day. My attempt at an explanation of this is merely to say that fish are more active and respond more completely to Solunar influence at this particular time. Until we know what Solunar influence really is, of what it is composed and how it can be measured, I am afraid that the full explanation will be impossible.

There is a decided similarity in the cyclic phenomena of the moon that has been well established. The annual appearance of the Palolo worm in the waters off Samoa and Fiji at the last quarter of the November moon is an established fact and its cycle is, without doubt, in rhythm with the moon, yet this rhythmic behavior has never been explained. The increase and decrease in the bulk of the sea urchin of the Gulf of Suez, this variance in absolute rhythm with the lunar month, has been admitted but not explained. These and other similar happenings continue to go their mysterious ways, year after year, but the solution of the riddle has yet to be found. Lacking the explanation and the knowledge of the exact cause, it is difficult to know where to draw the line between the probable and the improbable. Common sense tells us that beliefs concerning natural phenomena—home remedies and cures, effects of the moon, prognostication of weather changes and so on—that have been handed down from father to son through the centuries, would long since have been lost in obscurity if there were not at least some virtue in them. Surely, a home remedy that does not effect the desired cure soon will be discarded by succeeding generations. To last for hundreds of years it must, of necessity, be effective.

As much as time and opportunity will allow, I have been attempting for the last few years to secure and read the various reports of the work of scientists about the world, dealing with the effects of the moon on living things. Also, I have tried to keep in touch with the progress of research in terrestrial and atmospheric magnetism. One thing that impresses me as we go along is the pronounced lack of agreement among scientists who are occupied in the same fields of endeavor. To illustrate, I have today read the opinion of one scientist on the possibility of the minds of insane patients being affected by different phases of the moon. He expresses doubt about the actuality of any such relationship and says in part:

> ... whatever influence there be [note the use of the subjunctive, implying doubt] would depend on the phases of the Moon, that is, on a very short cycle. There is thus no opportunity for an accumulation of sufficient length to permit infinitesimal influences to become tangible.

That certainly is a direct statement if I ever saw one. Yet, right here in my file is a letter from the head of one of our large institutions for the insane. This is what he has to say on the same subject.

Moon Up - Moon Down

... recently I have noted that her mental condition has become markedly aggravated during that phase [the full of the moon]. Modern psychiatrists, so far as I know, are apt to smile compassionately at such notions but have never taken the trouble to check them up.

And there is the other side of the picture.

I suppose that in any matter that is as vague and intangible as lunar influence on the insane, there is bound to be disagreement. By the same token, research in atmospheric and terrestrial magnetism is progressing at such a rapid rate that some confusion is inevitable before the final establishment of basic facts. It is all very interesting but not very helpful in working out my own particular problem.

In the past, we, Beth and I, were hopeful that one of the universities or scientific institutions would lend a hand in finding the cause of the reaction to Solunar periods. It may be that this will happen sometime in the future. So far, however, they seem to have their own axes to grind. At the present writing, a large share of them are encumbered with governmental work in addition to their own particular brands of research, so we suppose that we must be content to wait until matters clarify themselves somewhat. We know that quite a few executives, doctors and professors, who are connected with these institutions, use the Solunar Tables annually as an aid in their fishing. Some day our turn is bound to come.

For the past few years, one of the men in the Department of Biology of one of our Pennsylvania universities has been interested in the Solunar Theory. He is an ardent trout fisherman, one who ties his own flies, and he has found that the Solunar Tables actually do predict, more or less accurately, the feeding periods of trout.

Last fall (1941), while talking to one of his associates, a non-angler, he explained the function of the Solunar Tables and the theory upon which they are based. He is familiar with my belief that living things are stimulated electrically during Solunar periods and the idea had occurred to him that it might be possible to find out something definite about it.

It so happens that his friend has perfected an instrument that is a valuable aid to him in his forestry work. With this device, he is able to obtain a reading of the potential gradient of a living organism at any particular time. Perhaps that might do with a bit of clarification.

Living things have the capacity to store up within themselves the power to produce small electric currents, much the same as a storage battery holds within itself potential voltage or current to be called upon when needed by your car. This "potential" varies in intensity, according to the size and activity of the organism. Thus, with an instrument that is sensitive enough to measure this force, an experimenter can apply it to one tree after another of a grove. He knows what the potential of a healthy tree should be, even before he tests it. Trees that are not healthy, either because of disease or attack by insects, will show a *lower-than-normal* potential reading—just the reverse of what your physician usually looks for when he takes your temperature. The instrument is an accurate diagnostician for sick trees in addition to being a great time-saver.

Having learned that his friend would be interested in looking into the matter of Solunar periods more thoroughly, Biologist A wrote to me and asked me if I would object to having Biologist B investigate the Solunar Tables with the aid of his new measuring device. It so happens that Biologist B had kept a fairly contiguous, hourly record of laboratory readings during 1938 and, if I were agreeable, it would be interesting to check this record against the Solunar Tables for that year.

Naturally, I was elated over the prospect. I am always more than willing to have the Solunar Theory tested out in any fashion. Not only do I learn more of what to expect—and what *not* to expect—from it; outside experimentation serves as a counterbalance against any possibility that I may develop to deviate slightly in my own observations, purely because of the fact that I am doing most of the work single-handed. In this case, I was particularly interested because I had no substantiating evidence to support my belief that reactions to Solunar periods are prompted by variations in electricity or magnetism. Accordingly, I wrote to Biologist B, sending him all necessary data and thanking him for his interest in the work that I had been doing.

For over two weeks I anxiously watched the mails and, eventually, patience was rewarded by a letter from Biologist B, telling me of his investigations. He and one of his colleagues had checked through several months of laboratory readings taken from germinating corn seeds and, also, from live salamanders. While the readings were not completely in agreement with the Solunar periods, *in 75 per cent of the comparisons there was an increase in potential gradient at the time a Solunar period was in progress.* He went on to say that the coincidence, while not conclusive, was sufficient to be quite interesting and deserving of further investigation through experimentation.

That was decidedly good news. Viewed in the light of cold, hard percentages, the results of this investigation are, as he stated, not conclusive. However, in judging these figures there are several aspects of the matter that should be taken into consideration. In the first place, the tabulations were made by two reputable scientists who are associated with one of the foremost universities of New England. Neither of them was familiar with the Solunar Tables prior to the investigation; thus, there was no possibility of any unconscious interference by preconceived ideas or conclusions. The Solunar Tables for that year had been prepared and printed long before I had heard of *their* experiments. In other words, the only possible connection or relationship that one set of figures could have with the other is the common medium furnished by the phenomenon under investigation.

Also, it must be remembered that the intensity of Solunar influence always is subject to variation, evidently caused by fluctuations in atmospheric pressure. We have already seen that such fluctuations are accompanied by variations or, at least, a reassorting of the electrical status of the atmosphere. My own observations of activity of wild life often show negative results during adverse weather conditions. With these things in mind, the results of that recent investigation take on a rosier hue than they might have at first glance through the microscope of cold, impartial percentages.

As you may well imagine, we are hoping that this may be the entering wedge in the solution of our problem. At least, it is a start in the right direction.

CHAPTER THIRTEEN

W E FIND it interesting sometimes to conjecture about the various ways in which the Solunar Theory may be applied in future years. Of course, there is no way of knowing definitely what its scope may be, for the simple reason that we do not, at present, know why it operates and of what it is composed. The total of our exact knowledge of it today is that the activity cycle does exist and is followed, to a greater or less degree, by all living things; that this activity cycle is timed in the same rhythm as the moon; and that it quite probably is linked in some way with terrestrial or atmospheric magnetism or both. It is not improbable, however, that the Solunar Theory will have fairly wide commercial application with the added virtue of benefiting mankind, from the standpoints of both health and general comfort.

We have already seen that it has its commercial uses. The commercial fisheries have found that its use improves their daily catches. Aquarium owners have learned to save food and labor in raising tropical fish by following the feeding schedule. A collection of reptiles is kept healthy through the timing of its feeding schedule, and salesmen have found that their prospects seem to be more receptive if approached at the proper times. But that does not exhaust the possibilities by any means.

We know that groups of people are stimulated noticeably during Solunar periods. Why not put that knowledge to good use later on? Today we can condition the atmosphere in an enclosure so that temperature and humidity may be maintained at constant, favorable levels. Once it has been determined just what constitutes Solunar influence, it is reasonable to suppose that the conditions that exist during a Solunar period can be reproduced artificially. The atmosphere in our hospitals, theatres, public buildings and offices could then be conditioned so that the occupants of these buildings would be subjected to Solunar conditions so long as they remained therein.

In our hospitals, we know that the majority of deaths occur between midnight and dawn. This has been accounted for by the explanation that bodily resistance is at its lowest ebb during the small hours of the morning. That is no doubt true, but it doesn't mean very much; much less does it suggest a remedy, so that this concentration of mortality might be distributed over the full twenty-four hours of the day instead of having border-line cases subjected without protection to the hazard of the early hours of the morning. In addition, who knows but what the reproduction of Solunar conditions may have its own peculiar therapeutic quality? At least, it will be worth while to find out about it, once we know where to begin.

In our office buildings, it is probable that "Solunar

conditioning" would step up efficiency considerably. Certainly, the observations that I made of our real-estate department over a period of four years would bear out that statement. No longer would there be a variance in activity throughout the day. It might well be that the eventual result would be shorter office hours with no loss in work accomplished.

A few years ago, I was giving a talk on the Solunar Theory to a group of sportsmen in a small town in New Jersey. As a general rule, I confine talks of this kind to a general discussion of the application of the Solunar Theory to the outdoor sports, and let it go at that. On this particular evening, however, there was only a small group present and they were interested enough to ask questions after I had finished my talk. Eventually, the discussion worked around to the effects of Solunar influence on people.

During a lull in the proceedings, a man in the back of the room rose to his feet.

"I'm a mine operator," he said. "Over near Scranton, Pennsylvania, our mines employ from one hundred and fifty to two hundred miners, foreigners mostly—unnaturalized immigrants from the peasant classes of Europe. A good share of them are completely uneducated; in fact, they are closer to being highly developed animals than they are people, at least as we think of people in this country.

"When a certain number of these men is working in the mines, we know just about what output to expect from a day's work. A good share of the time, the men turn out coal as we expect them to and everything moves along according to schedule. But that is not always the case.

"Once in a while, usually when the weather is fine and the men are feeling good, this crew will send up coal faster than we can handle it. This doesn't happen often—just every now and then. Then, on other days, when the weather is gloomy and the men don't feel so lively, we have trouble getting up enough coal to fill our orders. Empty cars stand on the sidings and demurrage charges pile up. Often we try to hurry the men by speeding up the fans and forcing more air into the mines, but it doesn't seem to do much good. We either get coal or we don't get it, depending on how those fellows happen to be feeling from day to day. It costs money for power to operate those big nine-foot fans and it costs money to be late in getting out orders. I'm wondering if your Solunar Theory won't be the eventual solution."

It would be an absorbing bit of research to check the production sheets of those mines against Solunar periods and fluctuations in barometric pressure. But that kind of work requires time and, possibly, equipment. In the event that it should develop that coal production actually does vary directly as the Solunar periods and the barograph (as it quite probably does), we still lack the remedy until we know enough about reproducing favorable barometric and Solunar conditions.

This unexplained variance in group efficiency is not confined to coal mines. The same fluctuation in output is evident in every form of manufacture not entirely dependent upon machinery.

Some years ago, I gave a luncheon talk to the Rotary Club at Flint, Michigan. At the close of the session, a man came up to the speakers' table and introduced himself. He explained that he was the superintendent of the assembly line of one of the automobile-manufacturing plants in Flint.

"You probably know," he said, "that we try to maintain standard working conditions in assembly-line work from day to day. Each man has his regular job to do. He does just that one job, in the same place, with the same tools, time after time, day after day. We try to have conditions in the plant as uniform as possible—light, heat and so on. Yet, try as we will, we can't maintain an even production rate. Some days we speed up the line until cars roll off faster than the loading crew can handle them. Other days, we have to slow down the assembly line, sometimes stopping it until some of the men can catch up, while the loading crew stands around, waiting for something to do.

"As you might imagine, a graph of our production from day to day over a period of months is far from being the straight line that we should like to see. We never change a man on the assembly line if we can help it. It's the same crew working on the good days and the bad days. But the variance in production persists in spite of our efforts to eliminate it. I tell you, it keeps me awake nights sometimes."

That seems to sum up the need for a remedy for variance in production. The automobile industry is noted for having the last word in factory arrangement, manufacturing methods and efficient tools. Yet, when dealing with the unknown quantity of manual efficiency, production schedules can and often do, go completely awry. Were it possible to condition a modern manufacturing plant so that, in addition to light, heat and humidity, the other variable working conditions—those of atmospheric pressure and Solunar influence, with their attendant magnetic fluctuations—could be kept at a standard level, it undoubtedly would result in more uniform production with its resultant economies.

Pending the time, however, that the fund of human information will permit such a stabilization of conditions, the Solunar Theory may not be without some practical value, just as it stands today. Only recently, I received a letter from a man who is a prominent surgeon in the Middle West. In this letter is the following:

> May I hope that our correspondence will continue as I have a kindred interest so far as human beings are concerned as you have in animals. I am sure you can see at once the great value it [the accurate forecast of Solunar periods] would have, when crystallized, in timing surgery, a fore-warning of heart failure, asthmatic attacks and so forth, if presented on a practical basis.

My reply to this letter was to the effect that, lacking definite knowledge as to cause, our only method of determining Solunar periods is through observation of known effects and their correlation with the known rhythms of the moon and sun. True, this is far from being a satisfactory method of calculation, but it is the best one we have at present.

On the other hand, diagnosis and surgery are carried on today with no thought of the Solunar Theory or the possible effects of the Solunar periods. Surely there is little to be lost if the Solunar Theory were taken into consideration when plans for operations are being made and when border-line cases are under observation and treatment.

The fact remains, however, that the effects of Solunar influence do show up in skeet scores, golf scores, etc. With this in mind, it could do no possible harm if any form of human endeavor, requiring keen co-ordination or judgment, were planned to take advantage of the stimulation of the Solunar periods. Directors' meetings, business conferences, surgical operations, theatrical performances and so on, indefinitely, might, just as well as not, profit from the beneficial results of Solunar influence. It is there to be used by those who want it—any school of trout or covey of quail will tell you that. Why, then, not take advantage of what nature has to offer?

It may be that the calendar on your desk ten years from the time that this is written will include not only the days of the month but the daily Solunar periods as well, with such additional related data as may be developed in the meanwhile. That time is probably a long way off, but it's fun to think about it, anyway.

CHAPTER FOURTEEN

LOOKING back over the years, the thought is brought home to me that so often it is the small things in the experience of most of us that tilt the balance of our lives one way or the other. That memorable fishing trip with Bob Wall in the labyrinthian maze of the St. Johns marshes in Florida fifteen years ago most certainly has left its mark on my life and that of my family. One thing leads to another, inevitably. What was once an interesting side light of my hobby of fishing has changed the entire course of our lives, without doubt. Had it not been for the extra work that I imposed upon myself, working out the complexities of the Solunar Theory and, later, developing the sale of Solunar Tables into a full-time business, I probably would still be working in the Real Estate Department in a large New York bank or, for all that I know, I might be dead and buried by this time. Thank Heaven, and I speak in all reverence, Bob Wall's rule of fishing, as taught to him by his "granpappy" many years ago in Georgia, proved to be my "Emancipation Proclamation," whereby I was freed from a life of secure drudgery and boredom. No longer is it incumbent upon me to punch the clock each morning at an exact time if I would continue to hold my job. We live our own lives now, and that alone is worth much sacrifice.

Before we branched out on our own, such a thing as contiguous observation of wild life was out of the question. My duties at the bank permitted fishing trips only every other week-end and my hunting trips were limited to two a season. Now, living in the heart of a fishing and hunting country, I can, if I choose, spend part or all of each day in the outdoors. From the 15th of April until the close of the bird season at the end of November, I live most of my life in the open. Beth no longer is held down to routine household duties, purely because we make a point of having no routine. Meals are eaten when we want them, not when the clock tells us to have them.

Even with my boy Dick life goes on more pleasantly than before. Being far removed from the hazards of metropolitan congestion, he is allowed more freedom than he could have enjoyed under the old regime. In view of the fact that he has planned his schooling to fit the work that we are doing, we have been able to arrange for time off from school without truant penalties. The faculty, knowing that fishing and shooting are essential in his future work as an outdoor writer, accept my explanation that a day's absence now and then falls within the all-inclusive classification of general education. We find that we spend much more time together under the present arrangement than ever could have been possible under the regimented existence.

Of course, we don't expect ever to be wealthy as a result of our efforts in bringing the Solunar Theory up to what possible stage of development it may eventually attain. Anything as intangible as response to Solunar influence is going to be difficult to sell to any appreciable number of people. Folks like to see things for themselves and often this is not possible with response to Solunar periods. Too many things can happen that will upset the fine balance of natural conditions to expect anything like 100 per cent visible performance. I write about the Solunar Theory and its effects and preach its gospel from the lecture platform, knowing full well that many of my audiences take what I have to say with a grain of salt.

To those who have not had experience with the Solunar Theory and its workings, all of the things set down herein may sound strange and, in some instances, fanciful. That is not surprising. The phenomena of nature with which we are not familiar and which we do not understand always sound implausible when first we hear about them. On my own part, I recall not a little skepticism that day fifteen years ago when I sat in the shade of a camphor tree and listened to Bob Wall unfold the lore of the Georgia market hunters. The story sounded strange to me then and I labeled it, mentally, a colorful piece of backwoods sophistry. It took a few years of personal investigation for me to convince myself that the fundamental idea is sound. How, then, can I expect, through the medium of mere words, to convince others that what I tell them is true?

But money is not all there is to be had in this world of ours. We have had money—plenty of it—twice in our lives, and we were none the happier for it. True, we could do more, gratify more whims and live on a more grandiose scale, but the fact remains that we are happier now than we were then. We are in the process of doing what we hope will be an important task of creative endeavor. We are interested, actively and keenly, in what each day has in store for us and, as time passes, the rewards of accomplishment are enough to satisfy us. What more of life can a man ask than to be happy with his family, interested to the point of absorption in his daily work and content in the knowledge that with his passing the world may be slightly better for his having lived upon it for a while? Although we can never hope to repay in kind the fun that we have had and will have out of life, at least we can try.

Now and then, some of our reward comes to us, perhaps, a little ahead of time. Some time ago, I received a letter from Arizona. It needs no explanation and I reproduce it here, in part, just as we received it. This is the letter.

> I've pretty well done my bit of fishing too—but one never gets enough. For the past two and one-half years, bum lungs have made an armchair angler of me. I have read everything I could get my hands on for a good many years and quite naturally I met you and your Solunar theory in the outdoor magazines. After my illness I found that an hour or so would be rather long for me to fish, so I thought, "Well, I'm going to try out this fellow's Solunar Theory." I ordered the Tables and started checking and studying them. Finally came trout season.
> My wife drove me the hundred miles to the little

stream. We arrived during a Major Period. The wind was blowing hard and the water was high and milky, but in approximately one hundred yards I raised seventeen trout. This was on hard-fished public waters and a small stream at that. This looked pretty good to me but I thought, "Well, maybe it just happened." Next morning I went out on a Minor Period and caught three rather small rainbows. Back to the house, for I must rest.

While waiting for the Major Period on a cot on the farmhouse porch—asleep in fact—I was awakened by the activity of songbirds, domestic fowls and turkeys. I called to my wife. "It's time to go." "How do you know?" she answered. "Listen to the birds," I said. "See how active they are—the squirrels too." I looked at my watch and the Major Period had just started. We hurried to the stream and I caught during the Major Period, twenty-six trout. Not bad for a man who was limited to two hours a day.

My health did not permit me to fish again last year except twice for bass near home and the Tables stood me in good stead again. I have carefully checked my Tables against various animals and birds which are around my house. There are hundreds of songbirds and I could tell when the Solunar Period started and ended by their activity.

I am really trying to show you just how valuable your Table is to a man who, on account of his health, can only fish an hour or so a day and must make the most of that time. There must be several thousand men in the same condition who would be able to get the most from their hunting and fishing if they but knew. To a non-angler this would sound extremely foolish but, to a man who has always been active and hunted and fished hard all his life, giving up these things is just about the hardest of all—no wonder then the hour or two is priceless.

Every once in a while, when my calculations have led me astray or my plans have gone wrong, as they often do, I take this letter out of my file and read it again. The gratitude and appreciation of this one man can more than offset the frustrations and disappointments that must be incidental to a job of this sort.

Unfortunately, not all of my readers—and listeners—are as charitable as this man is. A few years ago, I had the dubious pleasure of addressing a fly-casting club in one of our larger cities. It is a large organization and in its membership are several nationally known figures in the angling world. I did my best to give an interesting and convincing talk, and they listened attentively. Not until two years later did I learn how my talk really had been received.

After the two years had passed, I received a note from the chairman of the entertainment committee of that same club, asking me to address the club again at its annual dinner. The writer of that note never will be hanged for his diplomacy or tact.

"Of course," he said, "most of the boys think that your stuff is a lot of boloney, but I'd like to have you come over and give them a talk anyway."

My first impulse was to accept the invitation and go over to their dinner and give them a talk that they'd really remember. Then discretion—and Beth—stepped in and I declined the invitation and let it go at that.

In writing this account, believe me when I say that I

have tried to treat the matter of the Solunar Theory fairly and impartially. Throughout I have endeavored to separate fact from theory. Some things I know are true and those I have labeled as the truth. Other things are theory only and there is no hesitancy on my part to admit that they are unproven and, possibly, unprovable. In all things, however, I have tried to convey the impression that the work we are doing and hope to do is both serious and sincere. It is not, as that diplomat phrased it, "a lot of boloney." A man does not devote the useful years of his life to the creation of what he himself believes to be a fallacy.

And so, as I write these things, memory takes me back to the luncheon I had with the scientist who is prominent in the field of research in terrestrial magnetism.

"Go ahead as you are going," he said. "At least, you are on the right track. Stick to your guns and don't be influenced by any criticism. After you fuss around with it long enough, I'm sure you will find the answer and, more important, be able to prove it."

I think I'll muddle through for a while longer. Who knows what may develop?

AFTERWORD

During the thirty years that have passed since the preceding book was published, much has happened with - and through - the Solunar Theory.

John Alden Knight, who died in 1966 during his annual fishing trip to his favorite Florida Bay waters, lived to see his belief in the old market hunters' timetable vindicated. He, and thousands of others, demonstrated time and time again the efficiency of the Tables he printed annually. (One of his records still stands as of this writing; the Metropolitan Miami Tournament all-time sea trout record on fly, an 8 pound 13 oz. fish taken on the dark of the moon Major Period.)

The Tables are printed in major Western languages - French and Spanish as well as English - and are available from the Australian sub-continent throughout the Western world. They are distributed to over 150 newspapers in the United States and Canada (and have been since 1947) by the Register & Tribune Syndicate of Des Moines, Iowa. They are also printed editorially in Field and Stream, a magazine which certainly needs no further identification.

One of my late father-in-law's predictions as to the availability of the Solunar Tables came true in 1964 (20 years, rather than the 10 he had hopefully projected) when the Vernon Calendar Company first introduced their Sportsman's calendars, incorporating the Solunar times on each day's block.

There are major fishing tournaments whose committees annually consult the Solunar Tables office here in Pennsylvania for the scheduling of their competitions. These tournaments are timed for the dark of the moon to assure (as much as is possible in such a variable sport as fishing) the best catches for the most successful competitions.

In re-reading the correspondence the originator of the Tables had with the midwestern surgeon that he writes of on page 155, it is interesting to note that there is at least one prominent surgeon who, to my definite knowledge, does successfully utilize the Solunar times when medical conditions permit. He frequently uses hypnosis as an anesthesia for patients with tricky hearts, and has found that they are more readily conditioned to the technique during the Periods. Also, when conditions permit, he prefers to schedule major surgery around the Periods, giving the patient the added benefit of what he feels to be quicker recovery. While only one surgeon's experiences with a necessarily limited group of patients can hardly be claimed as a scientific proof, it certainly is at least an indication that humans react to the times perhaps more then we originally felt.

In 1957 John Alden Knight was honored with election to the Fishing Hall of Fame in recognition of his contribution through the development of the Solunar Tables, sportsmanship and fishing ability. When Dick, the son referred to in this book, was elected to the same group a few years later, they were the only father-son combination in a most distinguished group. While Dick lived only two years longer than his father, during his lifetime he did much to help his father refine the original formula and prove its value in many parts of the world, both hunting and fishing.

It was by these two dedicated men that I was trained in the Solunar Theory and the computation of the annual Tables. Ten years ago I had my first lesson from 'the boss' in figuring the times. He was a firm and fine teacher - and patient! - at the desk as with a fly rod or shotgun.

I feel I have learned well; trophy elk and antelope, and pending International Game Fish and International Spin Fishing records for a 64 pound white marlin on 6 pound line, all taken on Solunar Periods, show that, I think.

Yet that which constitutes the Solunar influence is still not definitely and truly scientifically known. Work is still continuing, trying to pin it down, in such diverse places as Colorado and New England. This is, however, the work of a few lone individuals whose inquiring minds prod them further down the road.

Perhaps one of these days one of them will come to the end of the road and we can say, "this is it". Until that day, though, I shall continue "muddling through", as the book has it, knowing that more and more people throughout the world have seen the evidence of the Solunar Periods, even if they don't know "why".

Montoursville, PA	Jacqueline E. Knight
November 1, 1972	(Mrs. Richard Alden Knight)

Jacqueline Knight continued the research, education and promotion of her father-in-law's Solunar Theory until her retirement on June 9, 1997. On this date, Knight sold Solunar Sales Company, which publishes the Solunar Tables, to Jim and Linda Losch.

Although Solunar Sales Co. is still based in Montoursville, Pennsylvania, the Losch's have traveled to various outdoor shows held within United States. Through these shows, outdoor tradesmen, nature lovers and sportsmen are acquainted with the use and accuracy of the Solunar Tables.

Today, the Solunar Tables are now printed in Spanish and English. They are distributed to Australia, New Zealand, Great Britain, Spain and throughout North and South America.

The Solunar Tables also appear in over 140 newspapers through King Features, making it one of the longest running features. Field and Stream also continues to publish the Tables in their magazine. In keeping with the information age, Solunar Sales introduced a site on the Internet, www.solunartables.com, which made its debut in June of 1998. Through this site one can purchase the most current edition of the Solunar Tables, Sportsman's Almanac calendar and other Solunar-related products.

The Losch's continue to research John Alden Knight's Solunar Theory and Solunar Tables. Each of their expeditions provides information supporting the validity of the Theory and precision of the Tables. Testimonials from those who use Solunar Tables also aid in the research process. In this age of computers and electronics, the sporting world persists in the application of the world's natural phenomenon to guide them in their sporting quest.

Montoursville, PA   James C. and Linda J. Losch
November 21, 2001

570-368-8042